Influencer Marketing

Marketing

A Beginners Guide to Influencer Strategy

(How to Build Your Successful Personal Brand and Passive Income Idea Through Social Networks)

Matthew Garcia

Published By **Ryan Princeton**

Matthew Garcia

Influencer Marketing: A Beginners Guide to Influencer Strategy (How to Build Your Successful Personal Brand and Passive Income Idea Through Social Networks)

ISBN   978-1-7775324-6-8

No part of this guidebook shall be reproduced in any form without permission in writing from the publisher except in the case of brief quotations embodied in critical articles or reviews.

Legal & Disclaimer

The information contained in this book is not designed to replace or take the place of any form of medicine or professional medical advice. The information in this book has been provided for educational & entertainment purposes only.

The information contained in this book has been compiled from sources deemed reliable, and it is accurate to the best of the Author's knowledge; however, the Author cannot guarantee its accuracy and validity and cannot be held liable for any errors or omissions. Changes are periodically made to this book. You must consult your doctor or get professional medical advice before using any of the suggested remedies, techniques, or information in this book.

Upon using the information contained in this book, you agree to hold harmless the Author from and against any damages, costs, and expenses, including any legal fees potentially resulting from the application of any of the information provided by this guide. This disclaimer applies to any damages or injury caused by the use and application, whether directly or indirectly, of any advice or information presented, whether for breach of contract, tort, negligence, personal injury, criminal intent, or under any other cause of action.

You agree to accept all risks of using the information presented inside this book. You need to consult a professional medical practitioner in order to ensure you are both able and healthy enough to participate in this program.

Table Of Contents

Chapter 1: Build A Strong Personal Brand

Establishing a solid personal brand is an essential element in maximising your income by implementing successful Instagram strategy for marketing. In this thorough guide we'll look at the most important components and strategies to help you build your personal brand to connect with your followers, and generate significant growth in revenue through Instagram.

To begin, defining your niche is essential. Find out your special skills, interests, as well as the particular audience you wish to attract. If you narrow your scope and establishing your self as a leader in the field you are interested in and attract followers that truly appreciate your offerings.

It is essential to be consistent in establishing your personal brand. Be sure your bio, profile and other content convey a consistent image that is in line with your beliefs and is a match for the audience you intend to target. Make use of your bio to concisely describe your identity, the things you're about, as well as the advantages you can offer those who follow you. Be memorable and engaging.

Quality content is the driving element behind the success of your personal brand image on Instagram. Put time and effort into making visually pleasing and captivating content that showcases your skills and add the audience with value. Try different forms of content such as images, videos as well as carousels and stories in order to keep your content interesting and fresh.

Stories are a great technique for creating a bond with your target audience. Utilize your captions and stories to create genuine and relatable stories which resonate with your audience. They will become acquainted with the person who is behind the brand and build a feeling of confidence and trust.

Engaging with your audience is one of the most important aspects in Instagram marketing. Be active in engaging with your users through responding to their comments as well as messages and mentions. Engage them with genuine concern for your audience's thoughts, ideas or concerns. Interacting with your customers does more than just strengthen relationships, but can also increase the chances of them becoming your loyal customers or customers.

Hashtags are a key factor in improving your exposure in Instagram. Find relevant hashtags and include them which are compatible with your posts and your intended audience. Use a mixture of well-known and specific hashtags for your niche to boost the likelihood of your content getting noticed by potential customers. Participating in hashtag communities could assist you in connecting to like-minded people and increase the scope of your audience.

Collaboration with other influencers could significantly increase your visibility as well as increase your revenue. Collaboration with influencers from complementary areas to promote each other's material or work together in joint initiatives. Collaborations like these expose your brand's image to new viewers which can increase your reach, and generating more revenue opportunities.

Sponsored posts can be a great option to earn money for your Instagram profile. Partner with brands that are aligned with your target audience and beliefs in order to produce sponsored content. Be sure your sponsored posts are genuine, and provide real benefits to your viewers. Integrity and transparency for sponsored partnerships is vital to maintain the trust of your readers.

The advertising platform of Instagram offers excellent ways to target certain demographics, and increase the reach of your ads. Try out Instagram advertisements to advertise your product, information, or products to a larger public. Examine and evaluate the results of your advertisements to improve your marketing campaigns to get the highest possible ROI on your investments.

A major avenue to increase income generation is to launch your own store online. Make use of features such as shoppable posts as well as links within your bio to effortlessly connect your items or services to the content of your Instagram profile. Make sure that your products and services align with your brand's image and meet the requirements and preferences of your followers.

Affiliate marketing is another method to earn money through Instagram. Advertise products or services by using specific affiliate links or code and earn a percentage of each sale you make through the referrals you make. Pick products that match the brand you represent and are something people who visit your site would appreciate.

Webinars or live events provide exclusive and beneficial experience to your audience at a cost. Your expertise, knowledge and useful guidance in a live format which allows your viewers to connect directly with you, and gain knowledge from your experience.

Coaching or consulting in your field that you are an expert in can provide an effective source of income. Make use of your expertise and knowledge to offer individualized advice and assistance to those or companies that require your services.

Collaboration with local businesses could offer exciting opportunities to sponsor postings, product placements or even event-related promotions. When you partner with local establishments it is possible to tap into the customer base of their establishment and earn extra revenue as well as promoting companies that you truly support.

To maximise your potential revenue to maximize your revenue potential on Instagram To maximize your Instagram revenue, you must monitor and analyse your results. Use Instagram's analytics built into the platform to learn more about the demographics of your followers, their the engagement of your content, as well as follower increase. By analyzing these statistics, you are able to take informed decisions and refine your strategy and improve your content in order in order to get the highest possible outcomes.

Utilizing these successful Instagram marketing techniques by following these effective Instagram marketing strategies, you will be able to build your personal brand, draw your followers in to maximize your income potential. Keep in mind that your success in Instagram requires time and constant efforts. Keep your branding consistent and provide an experience to your customers and modify your strategies according to the feedback you receive and your analytics. If you are committed and have a well-planned strategy, you'll be able to tap the maximum potential revenue of Instagram and take your company or personal brand to higher levels.

"Optimize your Bio"

Optimizing your bio is an essential aspect of maximising your earnings with successful Instagram advertising strategies. In this guide to complete we'll look at the essential elements and practical methods to assist you in creating a captivating and profitable Instagram bio that will make your profile more appealing and engaging to your intended viewers.

Your bio is your initial impression, and serves as a portal for prospective clients and followers. Your bio should be clear about your identity, the things you're doing, as well as the benefits you can provide. Create a clear and engaging bio that quickly exposes your unique selling value (USP).

Introduce yourself or your business in a clear and memorable manner. Your expertise, your passions or your area of expertise work within. Think about incorporating a catchy slogan or slogan that conveys your personality as a brand, and grabs your target audience's attention.

In order to make your bio more interesting and useful add specific details regarding your services. In your bio, highlight the items, services or solutions you offer. Utilize descriptive language to convey what benefits people is likely to receive from your company.

Include relevant keywords that are reflective of your specific industry or field. This will make your bio more searchable and boosts your chances to appear on relevant Instagram search results. Find the most popular keywords in your niche which resonate with your intended users.

Incorporating a distinct call-to action (CTA) within your biography could significantly boost the revenue you earn. Inspire users to complete particular actions like making a visit to your site, sign to receive a newsletter or purchasing. Create a CTA clear, persuasive and straightforward to understand.

Incorporating a link into your bio is an effective strategy to generate visitors and generate revenue. Link users to your site your blog, store online or landing page so that users can look around your product offerings and buy. You can also utilize link shortening programs or platforms that permit users to post several links together.

Utilize the impact of social proof through including press releases, testimonials or noteworthy achievements within your biography. It builds trust and confidence by ensuring potential customers they're engaging with a trusted company or person.

Use relevant hashtags in your bio to boost your visibility. Find popular hashtags and specific to your industry that are relevant to your company as well as your audience. Include hashtags in your bio will help users locate your page when they search for relevant content or related topics.

For enhancing the aesthetic appeal of your bio You can consider using emojis to enhance your bio's visual appeal. Emojis add personality to your bio and highlight important points as well as break up the paragraphs, which makes your bio more readable as well as visually attractive. But, be careful with them and be sure that they match your image as a brand.

A regular update of your bio is essential to keep up with any shifts regarding your products, services or messages for your brand. Make sure it is current and up-to-date through periodic review and refinement of your bio so that it is in sync with the evolving goals of your business.

It is also essential to keep track of the success on your profile. Examine how your users interact on your page, the number of clicking on links, as well as any conversions that are generated from your bio. Make use of Instagram analytics tools or other third-party software to get insights into your profile and make decision-based decisions based on data that will optimize your bio to get better results.

If you optimize your bio by using these methods, you'll be able to make a memorable and profitable Instagram presence. Your bio functions as an entry point to your company's brand, and must be able to effectively convey your unique value to the people you want to reach. Be sure to constantly review and tweak your bio in line with the changing goals of your business and maximise revenue-generating opportunities through Instagram.

Chapter 2: Engage Authentically

Engaging with your audience in a genuine way is a crucial factor in maximizing revenue with successful Instagram strategy for marketing. In this complete guide, we'll explore the most important factors and strategies to help you create real connections, establish an authentic community and generate significant growth in revenue through Instagram.

Genuine engagement is at the heart of any successful Instagram marketing. This involves engaging with your customers in response to messages and comments, as well as cultivating relationships with your customers. Through genuine engagement it builds trust, loyalty and an underlying sense of community and ultimately, greater revenue potential.

The most important aspect of true engagement is to listen to your target audience. Listen to what they want as well as their desires and issues. Answer their comments as well as their feedback, queries, and comments quickly and sincerely. Make it clear that you appreciate the input of your customers and dedicate yourself to giving them the best value and assistance.

Engage users in meaningful discussions with open-ended questions that you can ask in your captions. Engage in the responses of users. Invite users to voice their thoughts of their own experiences, thoughts, or opinions about your work or the industry. It creates a sense participation and community, which makes the audience feel included and valued.

Be active in your community's posts in addition. Spend the time to share, like or comment on the content of their pages. Engage them in their life, accomplishments or struggles. It strengthens the connection between your follower and you to create a welcoming and engaging atmosphere.

The authenticity of your posts is essential to build trust and loyalties. Be candid about your personal experiences, or even challenges that you have overcome. It can be a potent method of connecting to your viewers at a deeper level. But, you must strike a compromise and keep your professionalism maintaining a sense of humour.

Answer direct messages (DMs) quickly and with care. Direct messages provide a safe space that allows your followers to communicate with you in person. Utilize this space to give individual advice, address questions or raise issues. Through providing valuable, one-on-one interaction and demonstrating your commitment to your clients' success and wellbeing.

Instagram Stories provide a unique platform for authentic engagement. Use interactive features such as questions, polls or sliders to entice your followers to be involved in the conversation and to share their thoughts. Integrate user-generated content through posting and taggining the stories of your readers. This will not only improve the connection with your followers but also enhances their voices and makes them feel appreciated and valued.

Live video is an additional effective tool to engage your audience in a genuine way. You can host live Q&A as well as tutorials or interviews in order to engage your viewers in real-time. Direct interaction provides immediate feedback as well as an atmosphere of intimacy and authenticity.

Establishing relationships with influencers from your field can increase the reach of your business and increase revenue. Work together on joint projects or cross-promote one another's content or host joint giveaways. Through tapping into one another's publics, you are able to present your brand to potential new audiences who might be attracted to your product or services.

Genuine engagement extends far beyond engagement on Instagram platform. Make use of other platforms such as Facebook, Twitter as well as email marketing or your site for closer connections to your customers. Give valuable content as well as incentives to encourage your fans to sign up for your emailing list, or to connect with you on different social media platforms. Multi-channel strategies strengthen the relationship you have with your followers and broadens the reach of your business.

It is essential to monitor and evaluate your engagement strategies. Keep track of metrics like sharing, likes and comments as well as DMs to determine what type of is most popular with your viewers. Recognize trends, patterns, and areas to improve. Utilize these findings to improve your strategy for engagement and develop captivating material that will generate the revenue.

Through authentically engaging your customers, you can create an audience that's passionate about the brand's image and ready to assist your initiatives that generate revenue. Make sure you prioritize quality over volume, and truly engage to your followers at a level that is human. Through building meaningful connections and building relationships, you can not only increase revenues but also build an ongoing and loyal user following through Instagram.

"Create High-quality Content"

The creation of high-quality content is crucial element in maximising your profits through successful Instagram strategy for marketing. In this complete guide, we'll explore the most important aspects and practical methods that allow you to create engaging and compelling material that will attract and convert the people you want to reach, driving huge growth in revenue through Instagram.

Quality content is the foundation of a highly effective Instagram marketing plan. It draws attention, connects with your followers, and establishes you as an authority within your area. When you invest time and energy to create outstanding content you will create a following that is loyal and gain income-generating opportunities.

Begin by identifying your intended people and what they prefer. Complete a thorough investigation to discover their interests, needs and issues. This information will help guide the creation of content and ensure that your content can be tailored to appeal to the specific demographics you target.

The visual appeal of Instagram is crucial. Instagram. Spend money on high-quality photography videography and graphic design to create amazing images. Make use of professional lighting equipment, techniques, as well as editing tools to record the best visuals. Make sure you have a consistent style to establish a consistent and easily identifiable brand image.

Engage your viewers with compelling stories using captions. Make compelling and engaging narratives to complement your images. Utilize storytelling methods to engage your viewers and stir emotions. Use relatable tales, useful information, or provocative questions that encourage participation and build deeper bonds.

The variety of your content is essential to maintain your viewers' interest. Explore different formats for your content like images, videos carsousels, Instagram Stories, to provide diversifying experiences to your fans. Each of these formats offers unique opportunities to display your talents, delight your followers, or provide useful details.

It is vital to be authentic when creating quality content. You must be honest, open and consistent with the values of your brand. Beware of fake or staged information that might make your viewers uncomfortable. Show real life moments, behind-the-scenes moments, or even personal stories for a feeling of authenticity and realism.

Informational and educational information is extremely useful to your readers. Offer practical tips, instructional videos or business insights to assist your audience in solving their issues or enhance their lives. Make yourself known as a trustworthy expert by providing useful information that increases your credibility as well as builds trust.

Engagement is a two-way road when you use Instagram. Invite users to engage through your posts by posing questions using stickers that are interactive as well as running contests and giveaways. Be prompt and considerate in responding to feedback, messages and mentions, to encourage genuine dialogues. When you actively engage with your followers it shows how much you value their feedback and value their input.

Utilize the power of user-generated information (UGC) to boost your strategy for content. Invite your fans to post their stories and testimonials or other work that relate to your business. Repost the content and tag UGC to highlight your followers and promote a sense inclusion. UGC is not only social proof, but it also inspires users to be ambassadors for your business, thereby broadening your reach and generating revenues.

The importance of consistency is in the creation of content. Set up a regular posting schedule so that your viewers are entertained and anticipating your information. Create and arrange your content ahead of time by using calendars for content or other the scheduling tools. This lets you maintain a the flow of quality content and reduce tension or confusion.

Be informed of the latest news and trends in your sector. Include trending hashtags in your content, take part in competitions, or post recent news and updates in order to keep your content relevant and attract the attention of your target audience. But, make sure that the trends you choose to use are in line with your branding and offer benefits to your customers.

Analyze the success of your content in order to determine which content resonates most with your followers. Make use of Instagram analytics, or other third-party software to gauge the engagement, reach as well as conversions. Review the information to find patterns, trends, as well as possibilities for improvement. Modify your strategy for content based on the data to improve the revenue-generating efforts.

If you consistently create quality content that is resonant with your intended audience and your target audience, you will build a solid following, improve the number of followers you reach, and generate an impressive increase in revenue through Instagram. Be sure to know your target audience and focus on visual appeal. share compelling stories, give quality content, and engage in your social network. If you take a deliberate and planned method of creating content, you can increase your profit potential through Instagram and enjoy long-term achievement.

"Use Relevant Hashtags"

Making use of appropriate hashtags is an essential factor in increasing your revenues with efficient Instagram strategy for marketing. In this thorough guide we'll discuss the value of hashtags as well as provide strategies to use these hashtags effectively, reaching the right viewers, boosting visibility which ultimately leads to substantial revenue growth via Instagram.

Hashtags are a useful instrument to organize and find posts that is posted on Instagram. They enable users to find specific topics or trends and locate content that is in line with their own interests. Incorporating relevant hashtags to your content, you will improve the exposure of your posts, broaden your reach and draw new clients.

For effective use of hashtags effectively, you must first conduct extensive research in order to find relevant and popular hashtags for your industry that connect with your company's brand and your target market. Look into popular hashtags, competitor hashtags as well as niche-specific hashtags, to gain insight into what your target users are searching for.

Find a way to balance the popular and specific hashtags. Although popular hashtags are able to reach an increased audience however, they are also subject to intense concurrence. These hashtags, on other hand, could not have the same reach, but draw more specific and active users. Use a mix of the two types of hashtags to increase the reach of your hashtag to an appropriate target audience.

Make a custom hashtag for your brand that is unique to your company or campaign. The hashtag you choose must be recognizable, simple to read, and aligned to your branding. Your audience should be encouraged to make use of the brand's hashtag for sharing content associated with your company's brand. It not only increases your branding, but it also lets you collect UGC or user-generated content (UGC) and highlight user experiences.

Make sure you strategically place hashtags into your captions or in your comments. Try different methods to determine what is most effective for your readers. Some people prefer to include hashtags in the caption some prefer to add hashtags as the initial comment. Whatever method you decide to use be sure that you use hashtags that are appropriate to the subject matter and improve the likelihood of being found.

Use hashtags that are short and concise. Beware of long, complicated hashtags which are difficult to find or locate. Utilize a combination of general and specific hashtags in order to attract a broader number of users, while maintaining the relevance. As an example, in addition to the most popular hashtags like #fashion, you can include hashtags that are more specific like #vintageclothing or #sustainablefashion.

Update your hashtag strategy regularly to remain relevant and uncover new possibilities. Keep track of trends, topics that are popular and discussions within your field. Change your hashtags to match the current preferences of your audience.

Participate in hashtag communities through active interaction via posts using relevant hashtags. Comment, like, or post content shared by other users on these forums to create connections and boost your reach. Through engaging with other users and gaining attention, you will be able to attract the attention of others and possibly convert them to customers and followers.

Examine the results of your hashtags through Instagram analytics, or other third-party tools. Examine metrics like views, reach and engagement to identify what hashtags have the highest results. Develop your strategy on the basis of the information you gather, and focus on hashtags with the most engagement and convert rate.

Work with influencers and other brands in your sector in order to take advantage of their existing hashtag communities. Collaboration with influencers that have large followings can increase the reach of your business and also expose your brand to potential clients. Make sure you use specific hashtags that are branded or used in campaigns within the collaborations in order to boost the engagement of your brand and boost its visibility.

Develop hashtag-based challenges or campaigns to increase participation from users and build buzz for your company. Make contests, giveaways or experiences that ask users to utilize your hashtags to participate. It not only boosts participation but also generates the content generated by users that can be utilized in the future marketing campaigns.

Use hashtags to enhance the captions of your Instagram Stories to increase their visibility. Utilize relevant hashtags as overlays or stickers in your Stories to attract a an even larger audience. Instagram's algorithm incorporates Stories when searching hashtags which allows you to reach out to different user groups, and boost your exposure.

Hashtags play an essential role to maximize your profits through Instagram to increase exposure, drawing a particular public, and increasing the reach of your account. With careful analysis, using a variety of niche and popular hashtags, interacting with hashtag communities and following the performance of your hashtag and performance, you can improve your strategy for hashtags and generate substantial revenue growth through the Instagram platform.

Chapter 3: Collaborate With Other Influencers

Collaboration with influencers and other influencers can be an effective strategy to maximize your earnings through efficient Instagram marketing. In this complete guide, we'll look at the benefits of collaboration with influencers. We will also provide practical strategies to assist build partnerships that are successful and reach new audience and eventually drive substantial revenues growth via Instagram.

Collaborations with influencers provide an unique possibility to tap into existing audience segments and increase the trust and authority of well-known celebrities in your field. When you partner with influencers that are in alignment with your principles and audience you will be able to increase your brand's reach, boost recognition, and generate the possibility of revenue-generating possibilities.

Begin by finding influencers that are well-known within your sector and are able to connect with the target market. Find influencers with the same brand style as well as values and the level of engagement. Review their posts, followers' numbers, and demographics to determine if they're aligned to your business goals.

Reach out to influencers using a carefully-crafted pitch that emphasizes the advantages of collaboration. It is important to clearly explain how collaboration will benefit their fans and increase profits for both parties. Think about offering exclusive discounts such as exclusive deals, affiliation partnerships that encourage collaboration. You can also encourage influencers to help promote your brand.

If you are working with influencers it's important to define clearly defined goals and standards. Set out the key indicator of performance (KPIs) including reaching, engagement, conversions as well as sales. Set out your goals and the metrics to ensure that the two stakeholders are on the same page and striving towards the same goal.

Create content in collaboration with influencers and make sure it is in line with their style and is in tune with their followers. Allow influencers to be as creative as they want but provide guidelines for maintaining the consistency of your brand. Create captions, ideas as well as images in order to develop content that is seamlessly integrated with your branding and message.

Think about different collaboration types in order to meet the needs of a variety of audience and goals for marketing. These could be promoted posts, Instagram sweepstakes, reviews of product, prizes, and collaborative initiatives. Explore different formats and determine what best suits your business and its target audience.

Alongside paid collaborations, you can also explore the possibility of mutually beneficial partnerships in which you are able to provide value the influencers for exposure. You could do this by giving them exclusive content, invitations to events or highlighting the influencers on your platforms. Through building connections and offering value to your customers it is possible to build long-lasting partnership that can continue to increase profits in the coming years.

Make use of influencer-generated material (IGC) to boost the reach of your business and increase engagement. Inspire influencers to produce material that features your product or services, and then post it on their social media channels to share with their fans. Post and tag the content to your personal account to demonstrate social proof as well as increase your brand's authority. This will not only present your company to a larger public, but it can also allow you to make use of the influencer's current group of followers and boost sales.

Monitor the effectiveness of collaborations with influencers by using Instagram analytics, as well as other measuring instruments. Track metrics like the rate of engagement, web traffic and conversion rates, as well as the sales that are attributed to campaigns by influencers. Review the results to find positive collaborations as well as places to improve. Make use of these findings to fine-tune your strategies and enhance the future partnerships with influencers.

Beyond collaborations between individual influencers you should consider joining influencer networks and agencies that link brands with influential influencers. They provide access to a carefully selected pool of influencers, and can facilitate collaboration. Utilizing their knowledge and resources, you will be able to find new collaboration opportunities to improve the efficacy of your influencer marketing strategies.

It is vital to be authentic in your influencer collaborations. Find influencers with values that align with your company's values and place a high value on lasting relationships over single-off promotions. Make sure that influencers provide real and authentic reviews or even testimonials. it builds trust and confidence among their followers.

In short, collaboration with influencers is a great way to increase your profits through Instagram. When you identify the best influencers and setting goals, co-creating captivating content and tracking the their performance, you are able to harness their influence and reach to increase your brand's exposure as well as engage with new viewers and boost revenue significantly.

"Offer Sponsored Posts"

Sponsored posts are an effective way of maximising your earnings by using Instagram marketing. In this detailed guide we'll explore the advantages of posts sponsored by advertisers and offer practical strategies to assist to create partnerships that are successful that generate revenue and grow your business through Instagram.

sponsored posts require collaboration with companies or brands who will pay to get promotions through the Instagram account. With the help of your followers and power, you'll be able to make valuable content that will promote their services or products as well as generate income to yourself.

The initial step to offer sponsored content is to build an authentic and credible personal profile through Instagram. Make sure you create content of high quality that is a hit with your followers and demonstrates your distinctive design, knowledge or hobbies. Develop a strong following and increase engagement by posting regularly with engaging captions and relevant interactions with your viewers.

When you've created your own personal brand and earned an extensive following, the brands start to be aware of the influence and impact you have. But, it's vital to stay on top of exploring partnerships to brands that are in line with your beliefs and market. Find brands you like and can be an ideal fit for your industry and provide goods or services you truly trust.

Engage with brands using a carefully-crafted pitch, which outlines the advantages to working together. In the pitch, highlight your engagement rates as well as demographics of your audience and the value that you bring to their branding. Display examples of previous collaborations or sponsored posts to show your capacity to develop captivating content and generate results.

When you create sponsored posts it is important to keep your authenticity and integrity. Choose products and services that match your own brand image and you are confident will offer the best value for your followers. The people you serve trust your advice which is why it's important to promote only products you trust and trust with complete confidence.

Make sure that the sponsored content is seamlessly integrated with the content you normally post. Write engaging and insightful captions that communicate clearly the benefits of the service or product that you are promoting. Use your personal experience to describe how the product or service has helped you and addressed the needs of your target audience or wants.

Quality images are essential in capturing the attention of your readers and increasing the effectiveness of sponsored content. Spend money on professional photography or design attractive images that showcase your products or services effectively. Create a consistent look to build your brand's identity and build a unified feed.

Give value to your followers through special discounts, giveaways or any other incentive on your sponsored posts. It not only increases participation but also gives an urgency that boosts sales. Work with brands on special offers that appeal to the audience you target and offer additional incentive for customers to buy.

Make sure that sponsored posts are clearly disclosed and openly in order to build the trust of your readers. Utilize hashtags such as #ad,"sponsored" or "paid" to show that the post is a collaboration for promotion. Make sure that the information is easy to spot and conforms to the guidelines for advertising set by the platform, as well as other the relevant regulatory authorities.

Examine regularly the results of your sponsored content to maximize your revenue. Keep track of engagement metrics, such as comments, likes, and shares, to assess how effective your collaborations are. Check your conversion rates, click-throughs or sales that are attributed on your sponsored posts in order to gauge their impact on the revenue generated.

When your influence increases you should consider establishing standard prices for your sponsored content. Find out your worth in relation to factors such as the size of your audience as well as engagement rate and how much effort is needed to produce material. Prepare to discuss negotiations with brands, while remaining determined about your value and what you can contribute to the relationship.

Alongside specific sponsored posts, consider possible long-term partnerships or programs for brand ambassadors. The extended partnerships allow an ongoing marketing of a company's products or services. They also offer additional benefits, including higher payouts and exclusive content or the ability to attend events.

Be aware that maintaining confidence and trust to your target audience is crucial. Choose sponsors and products which align with your ideals and the needs of your audience. Make sure you prioritize authenticity over financial gains since a authentic and trusted brand can provide long-term opportunities for revenue.

In the end, offering sponsored posts can be a great method to maximize revenue via an effective marketing strategy on Instagram. With the help of establishing your personal brand, actively seeking partnerships, creating genuine useful content, and analyzing the performance of your posts, you could earn significant income as you maintain the credibility and trust of your target audience.

"Run Instagram Ads"

The use of Instagram advertisements is an extremely efficient strategy to maximize the revenue you earn through Instagram marketing. In this detailed guide we'll explore the advantages of advertising on Instagram. We will also provide practical strategies to assist you design successful ads that increase conversions and increase revenue through the Instagram platform.

Advertisements on Instagram allow you to connect with a larger audience than your own followers, and interact with people who might not know about your company's name. Due to its emphasis on images and its highly engaged users, Instagram provides a prime occasion to present your goods or services as well as drive sales-generating actions.

In order to run successful Instagram advertisements, begin by defining clearly your goals for marketing. It doesn't matter if you're trying to improve the visibility of your brand, increase web traffic or increase sales, having clearly defined objectives will help guide your advertising plan and assist in measuring the success.

You must then determine your intended people based on the characteristics of your demographic and interests, behaviours as well as previous interactions with your company. Make use of Instagram's extensive targeting options such as the location of your business, age, gender interest, location, and many more in order to narrow your market and ensure your advertisements will reach users who are most relevant to your brand.

Design compelling ads that grab attention and are in line with the aesthetics of your brand. Utilize high-quality videos or images which showcase your product or services in a visually appealing and compelling manner. Include captivating captions, compelling images and call-to-actions that stimulate viewers to take an decision, for example, going to your site or purchasing.

Try different advertising formats that include photo ads carousel ads with video or Stories ads to determine which resonates most with your customers and goal. Each type of format provides unique opportunities to present your company's the story of your product, show off its features and create engaging experiences.

In determining your budget for advertising be sure to consider other factors, such as your goals for marketing, the audiences size and amount of competition you face in your field. Begin with a moderate budget and closely monitor your performance. As you progress, increase the budget until you learn more about your performance and improve the effectiveness of your advertising to achieve greater outcomes.

Utilize Instagram's ad targeting tools, like Custom Audiences as well as Lookalike Audiences, in order to connect with those who share a common interest with your customers. Through the use of data collected from customers' lists, website visits or users of apps it is possible to create specifically targeted advertisements that will resonate with those who are more likely be converted.

Make your advertisements more effective for conversion with Instagram's conversion monitoring feature. Set up your Facebook Pixel in your site to measure and track what happens to users when they respond to your advertisements like signing up for a subscription, purchases, or downloads. The data provided by this tool provides invaluable insights about the impact of your advertisements and lets you to improve your message and targeting to achieve greater results.

Continuously analyze and monitor the results of your Instagram ads by using Ads Manager as well as other analytical tools. Keep track of metrics like views and reach, engagement through rates, click-throughs, as well as conversions to determine how effective your ads are. Recognize trends, patterns and areas to improve, using this information to improve your advertising plan to maximize revenue.

A/B testing can be a very effective technique for improving your Instagram advertising campaigns. Test different versions of captions, ad content targeted options, and calls to action to determine the most effective elements. Always test and tweak to increase the effectiveness of your ads and increase conversion rates.

Retargeting is an additional method for maximizing your earnings by using Instagram advertisements. You can set up retargeting ads to connect with users who have already been engaged by your brand for example, website visitors or people who've engaged with your profile on Instagram. Through reminding users about your services or products to increase conversion rates and increase revenues.

Engage with influencers, or use UGC (UGC) for your Instagram advertisements to increase authenticity and credibility. Join forces with influencers who are aligned with your brand's values and who enjoy a large following include their content in the ad campaigns. Also, highlight UGC which highlights good customers' experiences. It also builds the trust of customers and encourages engagement.

Also, periodically review and modify your Instagram advertising strategy in accordance with the continuously evolving platforms and the latest trends within the industry. Keep up-to-date with changes, new features and the best practices that you can use to make sure your advertisements are effective and yield maximum profits.

In the end advertising on Instagram can be an effective tool to maximize the revenue you earn through efficient marketing on

Instagram. Through setting up clear goals in mind, aiming at the appropriate target audience, generating compelling ads, optimizing them for conversions, and evaluating results, you will see substantial revenue growth while achieving your goals for marketing on Instagram. Keep your eyes open, test new strategies and improve your strategy to keep up with the crowded Instagram market.

Chapter 4: Launch An Online Store

The launch of an online store can be thrilling using efficient Instagram strategies for marketing is vital in maximizing the revenue. In this complete guide, we'll explore the advantages of using Instagram to advertise your online store. We will also provide concrete strategies that will help you boost traffic, improve conversions, and see substantial revenue growth.

Instagram provides a platform that is visually driven with an extensive audience, which makes Instagram an excellent platform for showcasing your product to your intended market, and boost sales. If you implement the best methods, you will be able to effectively market your store online and make the most of the engaging group of Instagram customers.

For you to open your online store effectively, you must first define your ideal customer. Find out their demographics, interest and habits to adapt your marketing strategies to their needs. Understanding your customer base will assist to create and implement strategies that align with their wants and needs.

Develop a visually attractive and cohesive presence for your brand through Instagram. Establish a consistent style which reflects your brand's personality and ethos. Utilize high-quality images of your products and lifestyle images, as well as posts from users to present your products in a captivating and inspiring manner.

Make sure you optimize your Instagram bio to give an appealing and concise description of your store's online. Include keywords, and the link to your website within the bio. This will direct visitors to your website. Create a compelling bio that reveals your distinct advantages and draws customers to browse your product.

Create a successful strategy for content that blends informative and entertaining posts. Highlight your product's features, emphasize the benefits and features as well as create appealing stories. Utilize user-generated content and behind-the-scenes images, videos or even lifestyle images to establish credibility and engage your target audience.

Utilize Instagram's different features for maximum interaction and reach. Leverage Instagram Stories to share special offers, new product announcements or content from behind the scenes. Make use of features such as polls surveys, or swipe-up link to increase interaction, and bring visitors to your website.

Engage your followers frequently by responding to remarks, messages to the point, as well as mentions. Develop a sense and establish connections with your fans. Thank them for their loyalty and continuously seek feedback from them to enhance your services and the customer experience.

Integrate influencer marketing into your Instagram strategy to increase your reach and connect with new audience. Join forces with influencers who are aligned with your company's image and who have a an extensive following within the field you are in. Their recommendation and endorsements could increase traffic to your store, raise brand awareness and drive sales.

Utilize Instagram's shopping options including tags on products as well as tags for products and the Instagram Shop tab making it simpler for shoppers to locate and purchase your merchandise directly through Instagram. Be sure your descriptions as well as prices are up-to-date and you regularly update your inventory so that you can provide customers with the best purchasing experience.

Create Instagram ads that are specifically targeted at the audience you want to reach. Make use of the ad targeting tools to target customers according to their interests, demographics, or past interactions with your company. Create compelling ads that highlight your merchandise as well as clear call-to-actions that lead users to your store online.

Set up a solid influencer or affiliate program in order to enhance your reach and earn revenues. Offer incentives to influencers and affiliates to help promote your brand to their following. For example, you could offer special discounts, affiliate commissions or opportunities for collaboration.

Participate in collaborative strategies or cross-promotions in conjunction with brands or with influencers. When you partner with similar businesses and influencers, you will be able to reach their audiences, exchange resources, and extend the reach of your brand. Collaboration-based campaigns, giveaways or joint product launches could help in generating the traffic to your site and increasing sales.

Utilize effective SEO strategies for increasing your site's exposure in search engines. Improve your descriptions of products, titles and meta tags to include pertinent keywords. Get high-quality backlinks from collaborations with guest bloggers, guest blogging or even influencer partnership to boost the domain authority of your website.

Analyze and monitor the effectiveness of your marketing on Instagram with the help of analytics tools as well as tracking the results using metrics. Monitor key metrics like the rate of engagement, traffic to your website the conversion rate and the revenue that is generated. Make use of these metrics to fine-tune your strategy, find high-performing web content and then allocate your resources efficiently.

Keep trying new things and experimenting with the Instagram marketing strategy. Be up to date on new Instagram features, trends in the industry and the preferences of consumers. Always review your marketing strategy and make informed decisions and adjust your strategy to increase revenue.

In final, the launch of an online shop offers enormous opportunity for growth in revenue as well as effective marketing strategies could be crucial to the success of your store.

Through defining the target market by creating an attractive image, engaging your customers, using Instagram features, making use of influencer marketing, executing targeted ads and assessing the your performance, you will be able to maximize your potential for revenue and develop an online store that is successful by using Instagram marketing. Keep your eyes on the ball, adjust to changing market trends and always provide value your customers to ensure sustainable increase in revenue.

"Affiliate Marketing"

Affiliate marketing can be a potent method to maximize revenue with successful Instagram marketing. In this complete guide, we'll look at the benefits of affiliate marketing. We will also offer practical strategies to aid you in establishing effective affiliate partnerships that increase sales, and see substantial revenue growth through Instagram.

Affiliate marketing involves working with businesses or individuals (affiliates) that promote the products or services you offer to earn a percentage per sale that they earn. Instagram offers a perfect opportunity for affiliate marketing due to its aesthetic nature and its active users.

In order to maximize the revenue you earn through affiliate marketing for affiliate marketing on Instagram Begin with identifying the audience you want to reach as well as understanding their wants and interests. This will assist you choose the best affiliates that are able to effectively connect the people you want to engage.

Find affiliates that align with the values of your company and have an established online presence and have an audience similar to yours. Find influencers, bloggers and content creators as well as specialists in niches who have earned confidence and trust with their audience. Their support for your product or services will greatly affect your potential revenue.

Create a transparent and mutually beneficial affiliate plan which outlines the structure of commissions as well as the terms and conditions. Offer affiliates all the equipment and tools to market your product efficiently, including description of products, images tracker links, special offers.

Make compelling and appealing images for your affiliates to incorporate into their promotional campaigns. It can be high-quality photos of products as well as lifestyle images, and users-generated content that highlights your products' benefits and advantages. your product. Inspire affiliates to share own experiences as well as their recommendations in order to build authenticity and confidence with their customers.

Create transparent and trustworthy tracking systems for accurate monitoring sales and affiliate referrals. Make use of unique affiliate links, or discount codes for every affiliate to monitor conversions and assign these to the proper affiliate partner. These statistics will allow you to determine the success of your affiliates, and help you improve your strategies to achieve better outcomes.

Maintain constant support and communicate with partners. Inform them of the latest product launches, promotions deals, or any other information which could help them in their marketing. Provide assistance, respond to any questions they have, and build a an environment of collaboration that inspires and enables them to advertise your product effectively.

It is important to encourage affiliates to reveal the affiliation between them and the brand they represent when advertising your product. Transparency increases trust among their customers and assures that they are in that they are in compliance with the rules and guidelines for advertising.

Use Instagram's diverse options to boost the effectiveness of your affiliate marketing. Inspire affiliates to make interesting Instagram Stories, posts, or live videos that highlight your product and incorporate discounts or affiliate links. Make use of Instagram's swipe-up function (if there is one available) for directing users to web pages that are landing or products on your site.

Connect with your affiliates posts through liking, commenting as well as sharing their posts. Thank them for their work and create a sense belonging. It will inspire continued co-operation and inspire associates to advertise your brand more effectively.

Review regularly the effectiveness of affiliate marketing campaigns with the help of analytics and tracking tools. Analyze key metrics like the number of clicks, conversions and sales and revenue generated by affiliates. Find the most effective affiliates and campaigns that can replicate the most successful methods and to allocate the resources efficiently.

Incentivize and reward the top affiliates in order to motivate them to continue their advertising of your goods. Give greater commission rates, unique promotions, discounts or even contests with affiliates that will motivate affiliates to remain loyal. Celebrate and acknowledge their accomplishments in order to keep a positive and successful affiliate relationship.

Always improve your affiliate marketing strategy Based on the feedback of customers and information. Examine the conversion rates as well as the amount of revenue earned by different affiliates, promotional strategies, or categories of products. Change your commission structures promotions, materials for promotion, or strategy of targeting in order to boost revenues and conversions.

Keep in contact with your partners and solicit their opinions. Invite them to share their insights about their experiences, ideas, or any challenges they face while marketing your services. These comments can give important information that can help you improve the affiliate program you offer and improve the overall experience for affiliates.

In final the affiliate marketing platform via Instagram offers a great chance to boost your earnings by implementing successful Instagram strategy for marketing. When you choose the best affiliates and providing engaging information and content, using solid tracking methods, taking advantage of Instagram tools, encouraging collaboration and constantly improving your strategy, you will be able to boost your revenues significantly and establish a winning affiliate marketing strategy through Instagram. Be active with your affiliates adjust to the market's patterns, and deliver the right value to your audience for sustainable results.

Chapter 5: Host Live Events Or Webinars

hosting live events or webinars can be a great method to maximize revenue via Instagram marketing. In this detailed guide we'll discuss the benefits of hosting live events and webinars via Instagram and offer practical strategies to assist you in planning the event, advertise it, and run effective online events that increase the conversion rate and result in an increase in revenue.

Webinars and live events let users to interact with their customers in real time, share useful content and even promote your product or service in a direct manner. Instagram offers a lively platform with an extensive and active user base providing a perfect platform to engage and reach your audience.

For maximum revenue from organizing live events or webinars to maximize the amount of money you earn from hosting live events or webinars on Instagram Begin by setting the goals and expectations. Define what you'd like to accomplish from your event. It could be driving the sales, boosting brand recognition and generating leads or informing your audience. A clear goal will aid in planning your event and to measure the success of your event.

Pick a topic with a strong appeal that is compatible with your readers' desires and also addresses their issues areas. Pick a topic that shows your knowledge and establishes your business as a trustworthy authority. Effective and relevant information will draw attention to your brand and boost the probability of making a sale.

Design the logistical aspects of your celebration, such as dates, times and length. Be aware of the timings of your targeted crowd to ensure that they are fully engaged. Consider whether to host your event on Instagram Live or utilize other third-party platforms that work with Instagram for example, Zoom and Crowdcast.

Effectively promote your event to draw attention and encourage registration. Make visually attractive images or videos to promote the date and then share these via your Instagram feed as well as Stories and highlights. Make sure you use compelling captions, call-to-action as well as relevant hashtags to boost exposure and engagement.

Collaboration with industry influencers and experts to host or take part at your live webcast or event. Their involvement and support will attract more people and help establish credibility for the event. Utilize their influence to broaden your audience and boost the likelihood of revenue-generating activities.

Engage your guests before or during and following the event in order to increase the feeling of belonging. Invite attendees to ask ideas or questions they'd prefer you to cover in the live discussion. React to feedback, participate with participants in live chats and build a warm setting that encourages active involvement.

In the course of your event, present captivating and high-quality material. Prepare your presentation with a clear plan, appealing visuals as well as a concise, yet comprehensive presentation. Integrate interactive elements, such as questions and polls or even audience participation, to boost the engagement of your audience and provide a memorable event.

Promoting your services or products in a subtle and strategic manner throughout the occasion. Include relevant demonstrations of your products cases studies or stories of success into your presentation. Offer exclusive discounts or special offers for attendees to encourage them to buy something or complete the desired action.

Save the session for later usage. The live stream or webinar and reuse video content for on-demand and educational tools, as well as promotional materials. Upload the recorded content to your Instagram profile, site, or any other platform to keep earning revenue even beyond the time that your live session has concluded.

Contact attendees following the event, to maintain relationships and boost conversions. Make sure to send personalized thank you emails and provide further resources or even offer discounts for the post-event. Keep in touch with your customers and keep delivering value in order to boost the chances of repeated purchases as well as ongoing revenues.

Assess the effectiveness of live events and webinars by tracking important indicators like participation, engagement and the amount of revenue generated. Make use of Instagram analytics and web analytics as well as other third-party tracking software to get insight into the success of your event. Review the information to find points for improvement, and then develop strategies for future occasions.

Always improve and tweak your webcast or live event strategy Based on the feedback you receive and information. Review feedback from participants and review surveys after the event and examine the behavior of attendees to discover areas of strength and opportunities to improve. Modify your presentation, content promotions, and follow-up strategies to increase revenue.

To conclude, hosting webinars or live events through Instagram is a fantastic chance to increase revenue by using efficient marketing techniques. With clear goals and deciding on topics that are compelling as well as promoting efficiently, cooperating with influencers, involving attendees and delivering top-quality content effectively promoting your event and recording your event to use in the future as well as following up with attendees to gauge success and impact on the event, you can achieve significant revenues and build an effective bond with your target audience. Be committed to delivering the best value to your audience, adjusting to their demands, and continually developing your strategies for events in order to ensure sustainable results for your revenue.

"Offer Coaching or Consulting Services"

Coaching or consulting by way of Instagram is an effective option to boost your earnings with effective marketing techniques. In this thorough guide we'll discuss the benefits in offering consulting or coaching services through Instagram and give you practical tips that will help you to attract customers to build your profile, and increase your revenue significantly.

Consulting or coaching services are the sharing of your knowledge, expertise and advice with your customers to help them reach their goals or overcome obstacles. Instagram provides a stunning and engaging platform that lets you showcase your expertise, interact to the people you want to reach, and advertise your business effectively.

For maximum profit from the coaching or consulting you offer for your business on

Instagram Begin by defining the niche you are in and then defining your ideal audience. Find out the area of that you are an expert and also your audience that can profit from your knowledge. This will allow you to customize your advertising strategies and draw those who are the most suitable customers.

Design a distinct and persuasive image of your brand that conveys your knowledge and appeals to your intended audience. Make a visually attractive Instagram profile that highlights your achievements, testimonials as well as success stories. Make use of high-quality photos, captivating text, and appropriate hashtags to boost your exposure and authority.

Promote your coaching or consulting offerings with content that adds value to the people who read it. Offer tips, insight and practical advice pertaining to your field of knowledge. Design visually pleasing images, videos or carousel-style posts which effectively communicate your message. Engage your audience through asking questions, encouraging feedback, and answering queries quickly.

Leverage Instagram's many tools to show off your knowledge and establish trust with your followers. Use Instagram Stories to provide quick advice, behind the scenes glimpses or testimonials of satisfied customers. Make use of Instagram's IGTV feature to offer more extensive content like videos or more in-depth discussions about pertinent topics.

Work with industry influencers and experts to develop content, or organize Instagram Live sessions. Their participation and endorsement could increase the reach of your business and help establish credibility for your products and services. Collaboration efforts could be as diverse as joint webinars, discussions with questions as well as guest appearances on one another's Instagram accounts.

Provide a range of consulting or coaching packages for different clients requirements and budgets. Be clear about the types of services offered and the length of the contract, as well as the price basis. Think about offering free sessions, bundle packages or options for ongoing support to offer flexibility and appeal to a wider clientele.

Utilize testimonials and case studies in order to demonstrate your knowledge and the outcomes you've achieved for clients. Get reviews and success stories from your satisfied customers and include them in your Instagram profile, your website and other promotional materials. Real-life testimonials and positive reviews could significantly influence prospective clients in their decision to use your company.

Utilize Instagram's direct messaging function to reach out to potential customers to answer questions, or offer additional information on the services you offer. Quick and timely responses could increase trust and turn prospective clients to paying customers. Think about offering free meetings or discovery calls to learn about the needs of your clients and highlight your value.

Develop strategic alliances with other service providers, or firms. Partner with experts that offer products and services similar to your own but aren't directly competing. If, for instance, you're a coach for career development or resume writer, you can partner with a resume-writing expert or personal branding specialist. Partner with each other to promote their services and recommend clients for maximum the revenue potential.

Use Instagram ads to reach out to a greater audience and draw potential customers. Design targeted advertising campaigns that are based on interests, demographics and behavior to ensure that your posts get noticed by those that are likely to need your guidance or assistance. Utilize compelling imagery, succinct messages, and powerful calls-to-action for conversions.

Continue to take part in professional development and remain informed about developments in the field and latest methods. Take part in workshops, conferences or online classes to increase your understanding and sharpen your skills. Discuss your continuing education experience with others to position your self as a respected expert in your field.

Always monitor and evaluate your Instagram indicators to gauge the efficacy of your marketing strategies. Keep track of key metrics, such as reaching, engagement throughs, click-throughs and the conversion rate. Utilize analytics tools to gain information about the effectiveness of your website and adapt your strategy accordingly.

Offering the services of coaching or consultation through Instagram can be a profitable way to boost your earnings with effective marketing techniques. Through identifying your market creating a brand that is strong by providing quality content using Instagram tools, working with other influencers, offering a range of services, using testimonials to boost your profile as well as engaging in strategic alliances, using Instagram advertisements and investing in professional growth as well as tracking your performance metrics and metrics, you will be able to draw clients and build a reputation and see significant growth in revenue. Be committed to providing quality, adjusting to customer requirements, and constantly developing your methods to produce profitable revenue growth.

Chapter 6: Sponsored Content On Stories

The use of sponsored content in Instagram Stories is a powerful technique to boost your earnings with effective marketing techniques. In this detailed guide we'll look at the benefits of content sponsored by brands in Instagram Stories, and offer actionable strategies to assist you in creating attractive and lucrative partnership with brands, increase income, and see an impressive increase in your business.

Instagram Stories is an exciting and exciting feature that permits you to post ephemeral and sporadic material with your viewers. Incorporating sponsored content into your Stories, you will be able to maximize your influence, reach and engagement to generate revenues and build profitable partnerships with companies.

In order to maximize the amount you earn from the sale of sponsored Instagram Stories, begin by creating a solid and authentic image. Determine your target audience, niche and beliefs to attract companies that are aligned with your posts and are a match for the people you follow. Credibility and authenticity will have a major impact on the establishment of successful collaborations.

Choose brands that match your personal brand as well as with your target viewers. Do thorough research to make sure your brand's values, its products and messages are in line with your brand's content and truly benefit your viewers. Concentrate on establishing long-term relations with brands that show an genuine passion for your content and will be able to provide value for the people who read your content.

Develop a media or sponsorship plan that shows your audience, engagement metrics as well as demographics. Include cases studies, testimonials as well as examples of collaborations that have been successful to demonstrate your capability to provide results for companies. This can help you attract new sponsors, and show the professionalism of your company and its value as an associate.

Reach out to brands proactively, and reach out to their social media or marketing team. Create customized pitches that emphasize the way your followers and content will benefit your brand. Highlight your knowledge of the target audience as well as suggest creative and powerful methods to incorporate their offerings or content in your stories.

If you are creating content for sponsored posts for Instagram Stories, it is vital to keep integrity and honesty. Be clear about the sponsorships you have in place in order to meet the requirements of advertising and to build trust with your viewers. Find innovative and interesting ways of presenting your sponsored content in a way that blends into your narrative style, and is a hit with your target audience.

Think about using interactive features made available through Instagram Stories, such as surveys, quizzes, or swipe-up links to engage the audience and make them feel more engaged with your sponsored content. It can improve the user experience, boost the brand's visibility, and increase sales for the brand sponsoring it.

Be sure the sponsored content is of value for your target audience. Make sure you review and assess the services or products sponsored by the company prior to endorsing the products or services. The honest and objective reviews you write increase your credibility as well as build trust with your readers and result in increased participation and more conversions.

Find a fair amount of compensation for sponsored content looking at factors such as audience's reach, engagement rates and the degree of work required to produce the content. Consider different types of payment, including cash payments, free goods or discounts exclusive to the people who view your content. Make sure you choose partnerships that provide mutual benefit and are aligned with your objectives for the future.

Analyze and track the success of your sponsored content Instagram Stories. Track key metrics such as engagement, reach, as well as conversions in order to evaluate the success of your partnerships. Make use of the data to tweak your tactics and optimize your content and produce better results to both your target audience as well as sponsors.

Maintaining strong relations with brand partners is vital to maximising revenue from sponsorship. Encourage open communication, offer regularly-scheduled updates about performance and ask for feedback from brand sponsors. Through delivering value while maintaining the highest standards it is possible to build relationships that last for a long time and boost the revenue potential of your business.

In conclusion, making use of advertising using sponsored content Instagram Stories is an effective method to increase revenue by using successful marketing strategies. You can do this by creating an authentic personal brand, finding the right partnership opportunities with brands, creating engaging stories, keeping your content transparent in your content, engaging your viewers and negotiating a fair amount of compensation, measuring performance, and creating good relationships with companies, you will be able to generate substantial revenue and build a sustainable business model using Instagram.

Be committed to offering value to your users and creating meaningful partnerships to be successful over the long term.

"Collaborate with Local Businesses"

Collaboration with local businesses can be effective way to increase the revenue generated by Instagram marketing. This comprehensive guide we'll explore the advantages from working with local companies and give you practical tips that will help you establish effective partnerships, expand the reach of your business, and create an impressive increase in revenue.

Collaboration with local businesses via Instagram provides a range of benefits. This allows you to draw on their existing customer base, increase your visibility in your community and build a feeling of respect and confidence in your intended public. Through a partnership and leveraging each mutual strengths and resources in order to generate revenue, and both profit from the alliance.

In order to maximize the revenue you earn through partnerships with local businesses via Instagram begin by looking for possible partners who align with the values of your company and your target audience. Find businesses that compliment the products or services you offer as well as share a common audience. The alignment ensures that your partnership is both relevant and attractive to the target market.

Contact local businesses with an enticing value proposition in which you explain how your partnership will benefit both sides. Highlight the possibility of reaching an even larger audience, boost the visibility of your brand, and encourage an increase in mutual success. Make sure you highlight the unique benefits created by partnering with a local company as well as the feeling of community that it generates.

Explore collaboration possibilities, like hosting events together and cross-promoting one another's goods and services or providing discounted packages or discounts to customers who share a common interest. Come up with creative solutions that will bring value to both companies and are a hit with your intended customers. The more creative and original your collaboration, the greater likelihood of drawing attention and making money.

Make compelling and attractive material to showcase your partnership through Instagram. Make high-quality photos, videos and carousel content which highlight your partnership and the benefits it brings. Make use of engaging captions, relevant hashtags, and calls to action to draw traffic to your site and get viewers to take the desired actions like buying something or going to the retailer of the partner.

Join in the sharing of mutual content by promoting each other's companies on Instagram. Highlight the services or products that your business partner offers in Stories or posts, and ask others to take the same approach in return. Cross-promotion exposes your company's brand to a whole new target audience, improve brand awareness which could result in increased revenues.

Organise events, or projects which unite both business as well as their customers and fans. These could include workshops, pop-up stores, or other community-based events to showcase the products and services you offer. Collaboration events offer the chance to reach out to a larger crowd, provide an unforgettable experience and increase revenue by boosting revenue or branding exposure.

Use Instagram's tag feature to acknowledge and give credit to the person who contributed to your stories or in your posts. Use the tag feature to mark your collaborator's Instagram handle and ask others to tag them in the same way. Cross-tagging allows your followers to quickly discover and learn more about the business of your partner which could lead to more customers as well as revenue potential.

Participate in influencer marketing through working with local influencers that are in alignment with your brand and who have a large audience in the local area. Partner with them in promoting your partnership through Instagram using their influence and impact to increase the reach of your message and draw attention. Influencers may provide authentic reviews or create compelling content and increase visitors to the business of your partner.

You can measure the impact of your collaborations through tracking the most important indicators like reaching, engagement the number of referrals, traffic to your site, and conversions. Utilize Instagram analytics, websites analytics or customized tracking links for insights about the success of collaboration activities. Review the information to determine the most effective strategies as well as areas for improvements in the future of collaborations.

Maintain and strengthen relationships with local companies even after the relationship has ended. Recognize the achievements and discuss the outcomes achieved by the collaboration. Keep in touch by engaging regularly on their website, taking part in events and events, or even connecting customers. Establishing lasting and strong connections will lead to potential collaborations in the future and generate the growth of revenue.

In final, collaboration with local companies on Instagram can be a great way to boost your earnings by implementing effective marketing strategies. Through identifying partners that are suitable by creating engaging content and cross-promoting, arranging jointly-organized events, participating in influencer marketing, tracking performance, and building connections, you will improve brand awareness as well as tap into new client base, and earn substantial income. Be committed to creating value, encouraging cooperation, and providing extraordinary experiences that will sustain income growth by leveraging local collaborations with businesses via Instagram.

"Track and Analyze your Performance"

Analyzing and tracking your progress is essential to maximising your earnings through successful Instagram advertising strategies. In this complete guide, we'll explore the importance in analyzing and tracking the performance of your Instagram account and give you strategies that will assist you in measuring the success of your campaign, gather valuable information to improve your strategies to boost revenue.

Monitoring and analysing your performance in Instagram is crucial for a variety of reasons. First, it helps you to see how your content resonates with your followers, what content is generating the highest interest, and also how your efforts are generating real results. Furthermore, it allows you to find areas of enhancement, detect trends and makes data-driven decision making to maximise your earnings potential. It also allows you to show the efficiency of your marketing on Instagram to clients, stakeholders or prospective sponsors.

In order to maximize the revenue you earn through successful Instagram marketing techniques, begin by establishing clear and precise objectives. Determine the key indicator of performance (KPIs) which are in line with your business goals including engagement rate or follower growth, web visitors, or conversions. The setting of specific goals allows you to measure your progress as well as measure the effectiveness of your strategy.

Use Instagram's built-in analytics tools, like Instagram Insights for access to important information about your followers the performance of your content, as well as engagement measures. Instagram Insights provides information on factors like impressions and the reach of your posts, visits to profiles web page clicks, and much more. Check these statistics regularly for insights into your results and take informed decision-making.

Monitor engagement metrics in order to assess the efficacy of your posts and engagement strategies. Track comments, likes, share, and saves to identify which type of content resonate with your readers. Study the components of your content like images captions, hashtags, and images which increase participation and then replicate these successful elements in your next posts.

Check the growth of your followers for a better understanding of the impact of your efforts to market increasing your reach. Review the demographics and interest of your following to make sure that your content is adapted to their interests. Find trends in followers' growth and engagement, to determine what motivates interest and loyalty within your followers.

Analyze conversions and website traffic for a better understanding of the efficacy and effectiveness of your Instagram marketing to generate sales. Utilize tools like UTM parameters, or customized tracking links that link visitors and conversions with specific Instagram content or campaign. Examine the conversion rate as well as the worth of conversions that are generated via Instagram to determine the ROI of the investment.

Use third-party analytics software like Google Analytics or social media management platforms to gain more insight on the performance of your Instagram performance. These tools offer additional information segments, advanced segmentation choices and cross-channel analytics which allow you to understand the overall effect that your Instagram marketing strategies in generating revenue.

Continuously assess your results in relation to your benchmarks and goals. Recognize patterns, trends or any anomalies which require your attention. Examine the effect of particular initiatives, collaborations or content strategy on the revenue you earn. Look for content, posts or collaborations that have had significant success and duplicate those strategies.

Use A/B testing to fine-tune your strategy and maximize your potential revenue. Try different formats of content including captions, hashtags and post times or call-to action strategies to determine the most effective strategies. You can split-test your content using different formats and posting methods, then compare their results to find which is the most effective strategy to maximize the amount of engagement and profit.

Make use of feedback from your audience as well as the insights gleaned through social listening. Keep track of feedback, comments, direct messages and even mentions, to better understand the preferences of your customers, their issues, and needs. Include this data into your strategy for content to give value, resolve issues and create a unique service that increases the revenue.

Analyze your competition's Instagram strategies and identify areas to enhance your own or areas that you are able to differentiate yourself. Check out their content engaging strategies, partnerships as well as promotional tactics to get ideas and stay in the forefront of trends. Analyze competitors to discover areas of opportunity or possible partnerships that may aid in revenue growth.

Record your observations and findings organized. Make dashboards or reports which track your KPIs and highlight trends and show the effects from your Instagram marketing strategies in terms of revenue generation. The reports will not just aid in monitoring progress, but will also be an important resource to use for future decisions and planning.

In final, tracking and analysing the performance of your account in Instagram can be crucial for maximising your profits through efficient strategies for marketing. Through setting objectives, using Instagram's analytics tools for tracking performance metrics for engagement, tracking follower development, and analyzing site visits and conversions with third-party analytics, measuring results against your goals, performing A/B tests, taking into account customer feedback, analysing competitor performance, and recording the results, you will discover valuable information, improve your strategy, and increase revenues to grow. Be committed to making informed decisions constant improvement, and providing benefits to your users for sustainable results via Instagram.

Chapter 7: Understanding Influencer Marketing

Is Influencer Marketing a thing?

In the current digital world the influencer marketing phenomenon is now a viable method for companies to communicate with their customers to achieve their objectives in terms of marketing.

Influencer marketing is the process of collaborating with influencers with an extensive popularity and influence through social networks.

The people who are called influencers, have developed a loyal, enthusiastic audience based on their individual brand, experience or their content.

The essence of influencer marketing is based on using the trust, credibility and authority of the individuals they work with to help promote items, services, or even causes. Instead of directly promoting to customers, brands work with influencers to develop genuine and relevant material that connects with their target audience.

Influencer marketing may take a variety of shapes, like review of products, sponsored posts brands, giveaways, mentions of brands or events that are hosted by an influencer.

What makes Influencer Marketing effective?

Marketing via influencers has gained immense recognition due to its efficacy in attracting and engaging the current generation of customers.

We'll look at the main motives for why influencer marketing can be extremely effective.

Credibility and Authenticity The influencers have developed the trust of their followers as well as authenticity fans.

The endorsements and recommendations they provide are viewed as authentic and trustworthy, leading to greater levels of trust for the advertised goods or services.

Specific Reach: Influencers are particular audiences, which are in line with the target audience of your business.

In partnering with influencers within your niche or field You can get in touch with and influence a relevant market that is most likely intrigued by the products you offer.

Increased Engagement: Influencers possess an uncanny ability to produce appealing content that connects with their target audience.

Their creativity, expertise and story-telling skills are awe inspiring their fans, resulting in an increase in engagement, comments shares, and likes.

Social Proof: When customers find their favourite influencers promoting an item or service this is considered to be social evidence.

Social validation boosts brand image and credibility, as well as encourages others to buy or test the products recommended by experts.

Enhance brand recognition by collaborating with influencers will significantly increase your brand's reach and exposure.

The large followings of their followers provide an opportunity for new customers to be introduced and expose your brand's message to customers that may not otherwise have heard of it.

Cost-Effectiveness: In general, influencer marketing gives a greater yield on investment than traditional channels for advertising.

The expenses of influencer collaborations depend on the extent of influencer's reach as well as involvement, however it's typically less expensive over traditional methods of advertising.

The types of influencers are Mega Macro, Micro and Nano

Influencers can be found in different sizes and styles Each with their particular advantages and disadvantages.

Let's examine the different kinds of influencers.

Mega-Influencers: Mega-influencers typically famous, experts in their field and social media stars who have thousands of fans.

They are able to reach a wide audience and have the potential to create significant exposure to brands.

But working with huge influencers could be costly, and their audiences could be less engaged as in comparison to lesser influencers.

Macro-influencers: Macro-influencers enjoy large followings, typically between 100,000 and a handful of million people.

They've established themselves as experts in their field and offer a balanced equilibrium between engagement and reach.

Working with macro-influencers lets companies to reach an even larger market but also maintain personal connections with their following.

Micro-Influencers: Micro influencers have very little, yet they have a large follower base, typically between 1,000-100,000 followers.

They usually specialize in certain areas and are able to create a more intimate connection to their customers.

Collaboration with micro-influencers is efficient and cost-effective. Their recommendations are often regarded as highly influential among their loyal fans.

Nano-Influencers are those with small followers, typically between 1,000 to 10,000 followers.

They are renowned for their honesty and involvement in the community.

Though their influence is limited but nano-influencers provide a specific and personal connection to their fans, which makes ideal for hyper-local or niche-based marketing strategies.

Advantages and Challenges of Influencer Marketing

We'll look at the benefits of influencer marketing:

Increased visibility of the brand and exposure to an appropriate public

Increased credibility of the brand and trust due to the endorsement of influencers

Improved interaction and engagement with intended group of people

A higher conversion rate and increased sales due to influencer recommendations

Access to exclusive and innovative tools for creating content

Cost-effective when compared with conventional advertising techniques

Opportunities to establish longer-term collaborations and partnerships

The ability to draw influencers knowledge and insight into their audience

Naturally, we also face challenges of influencer marketing:

Becoming difficult in identifying influential individuals who align with the brand's values and the target audience

Risks that could be posed by the controversy surrounding influencers, or with issues of reputation

Insuring authenticity, and making sure the contents are able to resonate with people who follow the

Measurement and assigning the influence of influencer-driven marketing on brand goals

navigating ethical and legal aspects, for instance FTC guidelines and requirements for disclosure

The balance of the budget allocation between influencers as well as other marketing efforts

Managing multiple relationships with influencers as well as coordinating production of content

Making realistic and achievable goals for your Campaign

To make the most of your marketing efforts involving influencers It is essential to set precise and attainable objectives. Take note of the following actions:

Establish Your Goals: Define your goals via influencer marketing. It could be raising awareness of your brand and sales, boosting web traffic or encouraging creator-generated content from users, be clear about your goals.

Choose KPIs or Key performance indicators (KPIs) Choose the most measurable indicators that are in line with your goal.

Examples are reach, engagement with click-throughs as well as conversion rates for followers on social media or the mention of your company's name.

Establish Specific and Attainable Objectives Based on your goal and data from the past, you can establish achievable objectives that you can achieve for every KPI.

Make sure that the targets you set can be achieved within the allotted budget and within the timeframe.

Take into consideration the Influencer Collaboration Criteria Find the minimum standards or standards that influencers must meet in order to join the campaigns you are running.

They could be a result of follower counts or engagement rate, as well as quality of the content or branding alignment.

Monitor and analyze results: Set up tracking systems and analytical tools to measure the effectiveness and effectiveness of your campaigns involving influencers.

Continuously review the data in order to uncover insights and implement the most of data-driven improvements.

With realistic objectives to measure performance of your marketing influencer actions, take informed decisions and constantly optimize your campaigns in the future.

The understanding of the fundamentals behind influencer marketing is vital prior to starting any program.

In this section we discussed the concept of influencer marketing and its efficacy and effectiveness, the different kinds of influencers, as well as the advantages and disadvantages of this strategy of marketing.

We also discussed the importance of establishing real-world goals that match the goals of your company.

Now that you know this, you're prepared to dig deeper into the field of influencer marketing, and to make powerful partnerships that boost the reach of your business and increase participation.

Chapter 8: Defining Your Influencer Marketing Strategy

Defining Your Target Audience

One of the most important steps to develop an effective influencer marketing plan is identifying your intended audience.

The ability to identify who your ideal customers will help you identify influential people with a meaningful and active followers. This is how to define the people you want to reach:

Do Market Research Begin with conducting a thorough market study to get a better understanding of your company's industry, its competitors as well as consumer habits.

Examine demographics, psychographics and patterns of purchase to determine who your prospective clients are.

Build Buyer Personas: Design specific buyer personas for each of your intended audience segments.

Stories or challenges, that offer innovative methods to connect with your intended viewers.

It's essential to pick the social media sites that provide the greatest opportunities to connect with your intended audience as well as align to your goals for the campaign.

An approach that is multi-platform could prove beneficial, dependent on the resources you have and your preference of the audience you are targeting.

Determining Your Budget

The process of determining your influencer marketing budget is the first step towards formulating your plan.

The budget you set will affect the kind of influencers who you cooperate with, the scope of your campaigns, as well as the amount of resources you allocate to the creation of content and its monitoring.

Be aware of the following elements to determine your marketing influencer budget

Campaign Objectives: align the budget of your campaign with its goals.

If your main goal is to increase brand recognition, it is possible to allocate a greater part of your budget engaging influencers who have a large range of reach.

If your goal is to drive sales, then you may spend more on influencers that have great engagement rates and proven track record in selling.

Influencer Tiers: Different levels of influencers have different prices.

Mega-influencers usually charge higher rates as do microand nano-influencers can be efficient in terms of cost.

Take into consideration the balance of the reach, engagement and budget when choosing influential people.

Partnering and Negotiation: Bear the fact in mind that fees for influencers can be negotiated, particularly when it comes to long-term partnerships and collaborations.

Prepare to discuss any additional benefits, compensation (e.g. gift cards for products) or incentive programs based on performance to maximize your budget.

Content Creation and Production Set aside a part of your budget to the creation of content and production.

This covers the costs for creating quality images video, images, or any other formats of content in conjunction with influential people.

Include any other costs for props, location or the professional services needed.

Tools for Tracking and Analytics Think about purchasing influential marketing platforms, or analytics tools to aid in tracking and measuring the results of your campaigns.

The tools they use can give you useful insights, and simplify the process of managing the influencer marketing campaigns.

Make sure to remain realistic and create an amount that is in line with your general marketing goals budget, resources, and anticipated ROI (ROI).

Making a compelling brand story

An appealing brand narrative is crucial to engage your audience of choice and to engage the influencers in a meaningful way.

A properly-crafted story for your brand will not only be a hit with customers but also motivates influential people to be a part of your company. Take note of the following points to develop your brand's narrative:

Create a Brand Identity for Your Business Clarify your brand's values and core beliefs the mission, as well as your unique selling point (USP).

Know what makes your company distinct from the competition and the way you would like to appear in the eyes of your targeted public.

Create Key Messages: Establish the most important messages you intend to communicate via your marketing influencer campaigns.

The messages you send out should be in line with the identity of your company and connect with your intended audience's hopes or desires as well as issues.

Develop a Consistent Brand Voice Establish an unwavering brand voice that is a reflection of your brand's character and is a match for your intended customers.

If it's authoritative, friendly or humorous keep the same tone across all channels of communication.

Display Your Brand's Values: Your brand's values should be highlighted as well as sustainability and social responsibility initiatives or involvement in the community.

Integrate these points in your story of brand for a clear demonstration of your commitment to generating positive change.

Write a captivating narrative Create a captivating narrative that embodies the core of your company and engages the audience and influencers.

Make use of storytelling techniques to establish the feeling of a bond and provoke emotions.

Create Creative Freedom: Allow influential people to inject their imagination with their personal flair when telling the story of your brand.

Set guidelines and provide branding assets. However, invite them to share their own perspective. This creates genuine and relatable information.

Congruity across platforms: Ensure your story of brand is the same across every social media platform and reflects the general marketing message.

The consistency of your brand helps strengthen your brand's reputation and improves your brand's recognition.

An effective brand story creates an excellent foundation for collaborations with influencers. It also creates an emotional bond with the target market which increases engagement and retention.

The establishment of Key Performance Indicators (KPIs)

To assess the performance and the impact of your marketing influencer campaigns It is essential to define important indicator of success (KPIs) which are in line with your goals for the campaign.

Here's how to set up efficient KPIs:

Affiliate with the Objectives: Be sure that your KPIs align with the goals of your campaign.

If, for instance, your goal is to improve recognition of your brand, the relevant key performance indicators could be followership, impressions, reach expansion, or even brand mentions.

If the goal is to drive conversions, you should consider KPIs such as the rate of clicks through, conversions or the revenue you generate could be more pertinent.

Pick Measurable Metrics to use: Pick the metrics that are able to be precisely recorded and monitored.

The social media sites and the analytics tools offer insight into a variety of parameters, like the rate of engagement, traffic to websites and conversions, videos views or shares.

Pick the metrics that best measure the effect of your influencer marketing campaigns.

Create Specific and Realistic Goals You can set specific goals for each KPI you choose.

They should be a challenge however achievable, based on the past statistics, benchmarks in the industry and the overall goals of your marketing.

The setting of realistic goals can help assess progress and help identify points for improvement.

Take into consideration Influencer-specific Metrics Alongside the overall campaign metrics, think about incorporating specific metrics for influencers to assess their individual the performance of each influencer.

These metrics may include audience quality, engagement rates, content quality, or influencer-generated conversions.

Keep track of and analyze the data you collect Use tracking tools and analytical tools that help you monitor the results of your marketing efforts involving influencers continually.

Analyze the data regularly to uncover insights, spot patterns and trends, then make the most of data-driven improvements.

Through the establishment of specific KPIs You can evaluate the impact of your campaigns to influencer marketing and track the progress of your campaigns and then make educated decisions on how to improve future campaigns.

A successful marketing plan for influencers requires thorough consideration of a variety of factors.

In this section we looked at the significance of delving into your ideal audience so that you can align with influencers who are a good fit.

The discussion also covered the steps of choosing the best social media platform, setting your budget, coming up with an appealing brand story as well as establishing the key indicator of performance (KPIs) to measure performance.

With these knowledge You can move on to the next step of your journey with influencer marketing using a well-planned strategy your place.

Chapter 9: How To Identify The Most Influential People

Selecting the right influencer is a crucial stage in the process of influencer marketing. Selecting the right influencers that are in line with the values of your brand are well-liked by their followers, enjoy a high level of engagement and who are able to reach the people you want to reach is crucial for an effective campaign.

In this article we'll look at how to identify the most effective influencers to promote your business.

Investigating Influencers and their niche

In order to begin choosing the best influencers it is essential to conduct an exhaustive study of your field.

These are steps that can aid you with the course of your study:

Find Relevant Keywords: Identify those keywords or hashtags that relate to your product or industry.

The keywords you choose will form the base of your study.

Utilize tools such as the social media search function, Google Trends, or Keyword research tools to discover relevant terms that are popular in your field of study.

Make use of Influencer Marketing Platforms Make use of influencer marketing platforms that give you access to huge databases of influencers from various fields.

The platforms usually offer filters for search based on user characteristics, engagement metrics, as well as content categories. This makes it simpler to locate appropriate influencers.

Discover the Social Media Platforms Find relevant hashtags, keywords or accounts that are niche-specific through social media sites.

Find influencers who regularly make high-quality videos and an active following.

Take note of the number of likes, followers, comments, and shares that they get.

Examine Competitor Collaborations: Study influential individuals who previously worked with brands or competitors within the same industry.

The analysis of these partnerships can give information about influencers with an affinity to your industry and might be willing to collaboration with your company in the future.

Participate in discussions with your community Join online forums or social media communities or communities that are niche-specific to find people who are engaged and respected in your sector.

Influencers with these names usually have a loyal and engaged following. They are an ideal partner for your business.

Conducting thorough research on your field, you will be able to determine influencers that have genuine passion for the field and will be able to be a hit with your intended public.

Analyzing Influencers' Reach and the degree of engagement and authenticity

If you've found possible influencers, you need to assess their influence, reach as well as their authenticity.

This is how to evaluate the influencers you follow:

Reach: Determine the magnitude of an influencer's followers on various networks of social media.

Although a huge following may bring more attention, it is important to keep your eyes on engagement rates. are likely to decline as followers number increases.

Examine the reach of an influencer by analyzing the number of followers or subscribers they have, site traffic or any other metrics that are relevant to the situation.

Engagement: Search for those influencers with an engaged crowd.

Find out their average engagement rate taking into account factors like shares, likes and comments and even saves.

Examine the quality of interaction, for instance genuine comments or discussions not just the volume of interaction.

Genuineness: Authenticity is an important aspect of influencer marketing.

Examine the content of the influencer to see if it is in line with their specific niche and connects with their target audience.

Find consistent messaging that is genuine, authentic recommendations and open disclosure of content sponsored by sponsors.

Influencers who are authentic tend to be more likely to retain their followers' trust and respect. their fans.

Quality of Content: Examine the quality of influencer's material, which includes visual aesthetics, storytelling skills as well as creativity.

Examine whether the content they are using aligns to your image of the brand and the standards.

Good-quality content doesn't just draw greater engagement, but it also improves your company's image by establishing a positive association.

Demographics of Audience: Know the characteristics of the audience that an influencer is able to reach.

Check that their followers are aligned to your ideal audience regards to gender, age as well as location and interest.

Find influencers with a followers who are relevant and active in the demographic you want to target.

Through analyzing an influencer's popularity, reach as well as authenticity and quality, you will be able to identify influencers that are most likely to make a significant impact on the people you want to reach.

Identifying the Alignment of your Brand's Values

Reach and engagement are crucial, it's also important to make sure that influencers with whom you work on align with your brand's goals and values.

Here's how you can find how to determine alignment:

Check Influencer's Content thoroughly: examine the content of an influencer's previous posts to determine their general message along with their core values, as well as the brands they've previously worked with.

Examine if their content matches to your brand's image the tone, values, and style.

Find consistency and authenticity in the collaborations they make.

Research their reputation: Conduct thorough background research about the credibility of influencers in their field, as well as among and with their followers.

Review, analyze or even mentions to verify there aren't any controversies and ethical concerns, as well as concerns about the person who is influencing you.

Credibility and authenticity are the most important factors in determining the influencers you choose.

Examine Brand Fit: Take note of whether the personal branding aligns with your own.

Examine if their contents and design are a good suit for your goods or products or.

A natural brand-to-brand fit will ensure that influencer's suggestions and endorsements appear authentic and are a hit with their followers.

Examine Audience Sentiment: Review the mood and opinions of the followers of an influencer's collaborations as well as endorsements.

Be on the lookout for positive responses as well as trust and engagement from their fans.

Influencers with relationships with their fans tend to generate positive brand association.

Through ensuring your branding values, you will be able to build lasting, authentic relationships which resonate with your intended customers.

Building Relationships with Influencers

The ability to build relationships with influencers is crucial to establishing successful partnerships.

Here are some ways for establishing important connections:

Connect and Follow: Start with following those influencers who you're looking to collaborate with via social media.

Engage with their posts through liking, commenting and even sharing.

This helps build rapport and demonstrate your enthusiasm for their job.

Personalized Outreach: Connect with the most influential individuals via customized messages or email.

Do not use templates that are generic and customize your message to demonstrate that you took time to read the content of their messages and admire the work they do.

It is important to clearly state your desire for working together and explain how this aligns with their knowledge and target your target market.

Bring Value to Influencers: Give them with convincing reasons to partner to your brand.

Make sure you highlight the value that your company can provide by offering the ability to access exclusive items, events or behind-the scenes experiences.

Explain how collaboration could be beneficial to both parties as well as the audiences they serve.

Develop Genuine Connections: The goal is to establish authentic connections based upon mutual respect and trust.

Take the time familiar with the people who influence you as well as their passions and the motivations behind them.

Participate in discussions, provide help, and be proud of the accomplishments of your children.

True relationships result in greater success and more effective collaborations.

Long-Term Partnerships: Think about establishing relationships with influential people who share your company's principles and who consistently provide the value you expect from them. These partnerships will allow for greater integration as well as the creation of a an authentic story around your company's image.

Keep in mind that the relationships of influencers can be built upon respect and trust.

The maintenance of the relationships between people is a continual process that requires constant contact, assistance and acknowledgement.

Negotiating Contracts, and Compensation

When you've found the most suitable influential people and have established connections, it's crucial to agree on contracts and pay which meet both of the parties' needs.

Take note of the following aspects during the process of negotiation:

Clarify Deliverables: Define the work scope and the deliverables to be expected by the influential.

Please specify the amount and kind of posts, content timeframes, requirements for exclusivity, as well as any other activities for example, appearances at events or blog post.

Compensation Models: Deliberate the models of compensation that are most beneficial for your brand as well as the person who is influencing it.

Compensation may be designed around a flat rate or cost per deliverable profit sharing, or free goods and services or some mix of the above.

Be aware of the reach and influencer's involvement, as well as industry rates in determining the fairness of the amount of compensation.

Disclosure and Compliance: Make sure that both parties know and adhere to the guidelines for ethical and legal compliance for sponsored content for example, those of the Federal Trade Commission (FTC) guidelines.

Examine how disclosures can be put into place and what ways the influencer as well as the brand ensure transparency and compliance.

Performance-based Incentives: Think about using performance-based rewards to encourage influential individuals and link their pay with the attainment of particular KPIs.

This can take the form of incentives, commission-based structure and rewards for achieving set goals.

Contracts and agreements: Create signed contracts in writing or agreements which outline the specifics and terms of collaboration.

Provide details about payment plans and deliverables. Also, include confidentiality clauses, rights to content rights for repurposing content, as well as cancellation clauses.

Get legal advice from a professional to ensure the compliance of your legal requirements and protect the interests of both parties.

Contract negotiations and the negotiation of compensation require transparency and open communication between your company and influential people.

Find a mutually beneficial agreement that takes into account the needs of both parties and establishes the foundation to ensure a positive partnership.

Identifying the perfect influencers for your brand involves thorough research, evaluation, and relationship-building.

In this section we discussed how to find influential people in your field and assessing their reach, authenticity, engagement and credibility in determining their alignment with your values as a brand, building relations, as well as contract negotiations and the negotiation of payment.

If you follow these guidelines You can build strong alliances with influential individuals with the capacity to increase the reach of your company's message and reach out to your desired people successfully.

Chapter 10: Designing And Executing Successful Campaigns For Influencers

Influencer marketing requires careful preparation and execution in order to get the best performance.

This chapter examines the most important elements to consider when creating successful influencer marketing campaigns, which includes preparing a creative short with clear goals and co-creating content that is engaging, monitoring compliance and transparency and managing the influencer relationship.

Making a creative Brief

A properly-written creative brief acts as a guideline for influencers to provide the influencers with an accurate knowledge of your brand's the goals of your campaign and requirements.

How to write an effective creative brief

Introduction and background: Start with introducing your company's brand by providing an description of the company's purpose as well as its values and customers.

Set the stage for their involvement with your company.

Goals of the Campaign: Define your goals and objectives to accomplish through your influencer marketing campaign.

If it's about increasing awareness of the brand and driving sales of products or even promoting a product, make sure that your goals are clear and achievable, quantifiable pertinent, time-bound, and relevant (SMART).

Key messages and brand voice Clarify the main messages that you wish to send in the course of your campaign.

The brand's voice and tone to be observed throughout the creation of content.

Give examples of words such as keywords, slogans for brands that need to be used in.

Content Requirements: Indicate the kind of content that you'd like influencers to produce.

It could include formats like Instagram postings, YouTube videos, blog articles, and TikTok contests.

Set guidelines for length of the content, pictures hashtags and necessary product references or other features.

Creative Freedom: In addition to providing certain guidelines, it is also important to allow influencers the freedom to express their own style and imagination into their content.

Inspire them to offer their own opinions and perspectives while remaining loyal to the values of your company.

Call-to-Action (CTA) clearly state your desired call-to-action to the target audience of the influencer.

If it's going to your site or making a purchase or engaging in a particular event, be sure the

CTA coincides with the goals of your campaign and can be easily comprehended by your people who are reading it.

Delivery dates and timelines Create precise timelines for content creation Review, publication, and creation.

Please specify when they should make submissions to their drafts of content as well as when you'll give feedback and the date the time when content is made available for publication.

Create realistic deadlines that facilitate a smooth and efficient workflow.

Compensation and Contractual Information Then, reiterate the information about compensation contractual obligations, as well as any non-disclosure or exclusivity obligations.

It is important that each party has the full understanding of legal and financial aspects of collaboration.

When you create a thorough creative brief, it provides influential individuals with the instructions and guidelines to produce material that matches the goals of your company and connects with the audience they serve.

Set clear goals for your campaign

Establishing clear goals for the campaign is essential to measure the impact and effectiveness of your influencer marketing campaign.

Use these steps to create concrete and actionable goals:

Be in sync with the overall marketing goals Be sure the goals of your campaign align with the overall brand's marketing objectives.

It's about raising awareness for your brand or expanding the reach of your brand or driving traffic to websites and generating leads or increasing sales, your goals for your campaign should align with the larger marketing plan.

Goals SMART: Establish objectives that are precise, measurable and achievable. They should also be relevant as well as time bound (SMART).

As an example Instead of setting a vague goal such as "increase brand awareness," create a concrete goal, like "increase brand mentions on social media by 20% within three months."

Take a look at KPIs: Select your key performances indicators (KPIs) which can help determine the success of your targets.

They could include measures that measure engagement, reach and click-through rate, conversions and revenue earned.

Make sure you align your goals to the appropriate KPIs for a more precise measure.

Historical and Benchmarking Data Use benchmarking information as well as historical performance information to establish realistic goals for the goals of your campaign.

Review past influencer marketing campaigns, industry norms, or your own data, to determine benchmarks and pinpoint the areas to improve.

Communications with Influencers: Share the goals of your campaign clearly to your influential people.

Make sure they are aware of the exact outcomes you wish to get from the collaboration.

This clarity allows them to ensure that their content is created and messages with the goals of your campaign.

Monitoring and Analytics Use monitoring mechanisms and tools for analytics to track the performance and progress of your goals for the campaign.

Review the data frequently to uncover insights, implement adjustments based on data, and assess the impact of your influencer marketing campaigns.

With clear objectives for the campaign by defining clear campaign objectives, you can establish a precise plan for your influencer marketing actions, and ensure they're aligned to the overall marketing plan and that they can be easily assessed for its effectiveness.

Co-creating Engaging Content

Engaging content is key in securing interest of the intended people and motivating them to take desired action.

Collaboration with influential people to create content will increase authenticity and the engagement of your audience. Learn how you can co-create captivating material:

Set Content Guidelines: Give specific guidelines to those who influencers about length, format as well as any necessary brand references or other elements.

The key messages are to be communicated as well as specific elements of storytelling that go with the voice of your company.

Use the influencers' expertise Utilize influencers' experience and creative thinking to create material that is resonant with their followers.

Inspire your children to share personal stories, their unique experiences as well as authentic suggestions.

This ensures that the material feels authentic and accessible.

Engage in Storytelling: Inspire the influencers you trust to create captivating stories that are in line with the brand's principles and resonate with their target audience.

Stories that are told with passion and enthusiasm create emotional bonds, and increases branding recall.

Give influencers story-based suggestions or examples that can motivate them to create content.

Integrate User-Generated Content (UGC) Engage the influencers as well as their followers to create UGC. (UGC) in connection with your campaign or brand.

UGC may include testimonials videos that unbox, reviews or submissions of creative content.

UGC provides credibility, social proof and also encourages the participation of viewers.

Utilize Interactive Content: Examine ways to use interactive formats of content to improve the engagement of viewers and increase their interaction.

It could be questions, polls, challenges and contests as well as streams that live.

Interactive content creates an atmosphere of belonging and makes it easier for followers to interact with the content of an influencer.

Keep Consistent: Make sure that content produced by influencers is in line with the brand's image the tone, message, and style.

Offer your brand's assets, style guidelines or templates to aid influencers with aligning their posts to your visual style and communications norms.

Review and feedback: Set up an opportunity for feedback to read and offer constructive feedback on the drafts of content that influencers submit.

Provide suggestions, advice and suggestions to make sure that your final product matches your expectations and is aligned with the goals of your campaign.

When you collaborate on engaging content creation using influencers, you tap their expertise and creativity to create content that is in tune with the people they serve while remaining in line with your brand's message and mission.

Ensuring compliance with FTC and Transparency

Compliance with regulations and transparency guidelines, like the ones set out by the Federal Trade Commission (FTC) are crucial to influencer marketing.

Here's how you can ensure the compliance of your organization and ensure transparency

Get familiar to FTC Guidelines: Get familiar with FTC guidelines and policies relating to endorsements and sponsored content.

Keep yourself informed of any new developments or updates that will be sure that you're in compliance with any lawful requirements.

Learn from Influencers: Inform influencers on the FTC guidelines as well as the necessity of transparency when it comes to their online content.

Give them resources, guidelines or other training material to aid them in understanding the regulations and obligations involved in divulging content sponsored by sponsors.

Communication Requirements for Disclosure: Be clear about your expectations with respect to the disclosure of sponsored content to the influencers.

The format, the location as well as the language used for disclosures by using hashtags like #ad, #sponsored. You can also include prominent and clear language such as "paid partnership" or "in collaboration with [brand name]."

Monitoring and reviewing compliance Review and monitor regularly the influencer's content to ensure that it is in that they are in compliance with disclosure rules.

Give feedback and suggestions If you think improvements could be made.

Create an open channel for communication in order to resolve any issues or queries about FTC compliance.

FTC Compliance clauses in Contracts Add particular FTC compliance clauses within contracts or agreements with the influencers.

Be clear about the responsibilities for both parties in relation to the disclosure of information and conformity with regulations guidelines.

Consult a lawyer for advice on the incorporation of legal and appropriate clauses.

Collaboration with legal professionals: Meet with lawyers that specialize in influencer marketing, as well as FTC rules.

They are able to provide direction as well as review contracts and assure that your influencer campaign comply with all legal requirements.

In focusing on transparency and compliance to regulations You can protect your company's image, establish trust with your customers, and create an ethical foundation for practice in influencer marketing.

Management of Influencer Relationships

The management of influencer relationships is crucial in fostering relationships over time and maintaining good brand relationships.

This is how you can effectively control influencer relations:

Regular Communication: Keep in frequent and ongoing communications with your influencers.

Keep up-to-date with their creation of content, how they perform and any forthcoming campaign.

Offer feedback, direction as well as support for to align your content in line with the brand's goals.

Honor and Show Appreciation Give thanks to influencers' work and importance they add to your company.

Recognize their accomplishments, emphasize their work, and publically honor their efforts.

Be sure to regularly engage with their content through commenting, liking, and even sharing.

Chapter 11: Enhancing The Impact Of Your Campaign

Marketing campaigns that use influencers have the ability to make a significant positive effects for your company.

To increase the efficiency of your marketing campaigns It is essential to increase their reach and engage.

In this section we'll look at various methods to boost your campaign's effectiveness, which includes using multiple influencers to boost your campaign, investigating social media cross-promotion, including hashtags and user-generated material (UGC) as well as hosting giveaways and contests and working with influencers on longer-term initiatives.

Making use of multiple influencers

Working with multiple influencers will boost your campaign's reach and involvement by tapping into diverse groups and audiences.

This is how you can leverage several Influencers efficiently:

Diversify the Influencer Tiers: Think about using influencers of different levels, like micro, macro, mega and micro influencers.

Every tier has distinct advantages that can allow you to connect with different types of the audience you want to reach.

Mega influencers have a wide-ranging influence, whereas Nano and micro influencers have more engagement, and a greater the ability to influence niches.

Select Complementary Influencers: Pick influencers that complement one another with regard to content type as well as demographics of the audience and specialization.

Find influencers with an inherent synergy, and who can enhance each other's message and without concurrence.

Control Campaign Messaging: Check that all influencers aligned with the campaign's messaging and the goals.

Give them a concise description of your key message and the desired results.

Work with influencers in order to prevent duplicate efforts and to ensure that there is a consistent storytelling throughout the collaborations.

Combining Different Content Formats Inspire influencers to produce various types of content like blogs, videos or social media content or live stream streams.

The variety of the campaigns keeps it lively and interesting appeals to various tastes and preferences of the audience.

Collaborative Campaigns: Consider the possibilities to collaborate on campaigns in which several influencers collaborate in the creation of content or in activities that are joint.

Collaboration-based campaigns create excitement encourage cross-promotion and increase the reach and involvement of many influential individuals.

Through leveraging influencers from multiple sources, you'll be able to expand the reach of your campaign, connect with a wide range of people, as well as increase participation and exposure for your brand.

Experimenting with Cross-Platform Promotion

Promoting cross-platform allows you to connect with a larger audience making use of different social media platforms and channels.

This is how you can explore ways to promote your influencers across platforms. campaigns:

Choose Relevant Platforms: Find those social media platforms as well as channels that are highly rated by the people you want to reach.

Think about platforms like Instagram, YouTube, TikTok, Facebook, Twitter, Pinterest, LinkedIn, or specifically designed for your industry.

Select platforms that are compatible with your goals for the campaign as well as your audience preference.

Repurpose Content: Improve and reuse content created by influencers for various platforms.

Make sure that the format of content and layout to meet the specific characteristics and needs for each platform.

As an example, you can repurpose long-form video clips for YouTube and short clips, or highlights to Instagram and TikTok.

Cross-Promotion: Encourage influencers promote their content across various platforms.

In this case, a celebrity may promote a YouTube video via Instagram using a teaser, or behind-the-scenes footage.

Cross-promotion can increase the flow of traffic and engage across various platforms, and helps create a unified image for the brand.

Influencer Takeovers: Create Influencer Takeovers for your brand's social media platforms or accounts.

Let influencers curate information, provide their insight or interact directly with your followers. Influencer takesovers expose your brand's message to an influencer's followers and encourage cross-platform interaction.

Pay-per-click: Think about using advertisements through social media to boost your influencer marketing.

Make use of targeted ads in order to target your ideal audiences and increase your visibility and the effectiveness of influencer partnerships.

Through cross-platform promotions it is possible to expand the reach of your campaign, connect with different audiences and establish the impression of a brand that is consistent on multiple social media channels.

Utilizing Hashtags as well as User-Generated Content (UGC)

Hashtags as well as user-generated content (UGC) can be powerful ways to increase your campaign's effectiveness and promoting people to participate.

This is how you can effectively use hashtags as well as UGC:

Make branded hashtags: Design distinctive hashtags branded with your brand specifically for your influencer campaigns.

Be sure the hashtags you choose to use have a memorable and relevant meaning and are in sync with the message of your campaign.

Engage influencers as well as their audiences to make use of these hashtags while publishing related content. This will allow for an easy track andmplification.

Trending and Industry Hashtags: Look up trending hashtags, as well as specific hashtags for your industry that can be relevant to your marketing campaign.

Integrate these hashtags into your website content for greater exposure and be part of pertinent conversations.

Make sure that hashtags you use are carefully chosen in line with your company's messages and values.

UGC Campaigns: Inspire the influencers as well as their followers to create UGC in connection with your business or campaign.

Encourage them to make and distribute content through your tools, taking part in challenges or sharing their experience.

Repost and distribute top-quality UGC for a showcase of authentic brand interactions as well as encourage participation.

Hashtag Challenges: Create hashtag challenges in order to increase audience engagement and participation.

Create a challenge idea and then encourage influencers as well as their fans to develop material in accordance with the challenge's guidelines.

Interact with your fellow participants by responding to their comments, liking them, or posting their entries to the challenge.

Influencer-Generated Hashtags: Let influencers to develop their own hashtags, which align with the goals of your campaign.

These hashtags may reflect an personality of the person who is influential and can inspire their followers to interact in the promotion.

Track and monitor these hashtags for a measure of the engagement of your followers and their the reach.

Utilizing hashtags as well as UGC to increase the reach of your campaign, increase the participation of your audience, and build an environment of shared values for your company.

Run Contests and Prizes

Giveaways and contests can be effective methods to increase the number of followers you have, as well as attracting new ones as well as creating buzz about your influencer marketing campaigns.

This is how you can run profitable giveaways and contests

Determine Contest Goals: Clearly identify the objectives of your giveaway or contest.

If it's increasing awareness of your brand or generating content from users and driving engagement or expanding the number of followers you have on social media set goals which align with the goals of your campaign.

Pick Relevant Prizes: Choose prizes that match your campaign, brand and your target market.

You might consider offering your own goods or services in exchange for prizes, or partner with other companies to offer attractive prizes.

Make sure that your prizes are in line with the value of your business and are appealing to the viewers' needs.

ContestMechanics: Design simple and easy contest mechanics that encourage participants.

Think about the mechanics of liking comments, sharing tags with friends, creating videos, or casting votes.

Make sure that the mechanisms are simple to comprehend and are in line to the platform's rules and rules.

Collaborate with Influencers and Collaboration with influencers for promotion contests and giveaways.

Make use of their influence and involvement to increase participation and improve the effectiveness of the campaign.

Invite influencers to talk about their experiences personally with prizes as well as highlight their value.

Promote and Amplify: Boost the visibility of the giveaway or contest on your company's social media channels including websites, emails, and blogs and various other channels of marketing.

Make use of influencers' platforms and their audiences to get the most the reach of your message.

You can consider using paid ads or influencer cross-promotions to boost your campaign.

Promote User-Generated Content by requesting the creation of content by users as part of the giveaway contest.

Invite participants to contribute articles that are in connection with your brand, your products or campaigns.

Repurpose and distribute quality UGC to engage users and encourage more submissions.

Giveaways and contests run by your company are a great way to create excitement, boost the number of people who participate, as well as expand your campaigns reach.

It stimulates the participation of customers and rewards them for their loyalty and creates an experience that is positive for the brand.

Working with Influencers in Lang-Term Campaigns

The long-term relationships with influential people can prove extremely beneficial to your business, providing more brand integration, continuous collaborations and a greater branding affinity.

Chapter 12: Measurement And Analysis Of Campaign Performance

The ability to measure and analyze the results of your influencer marketing campaign is crucial for assessing their efficacy, identifying points for improvement and taking data-driven decision making.

In this section we'll look at the essential steps to follow when monitoring and analysing the performance of campaigns, such as defining relevant metrics as well as KPIs. Key indicator of performance (KPIs) using tools to monitor and track results, studying information and gaining information, making optimizations based on data and quantifying returns on investment (ROI).

The definition of relevant metrics and KPIs

The definition of pertinent measurements and the key performance indicators (KPIs) is essential to evaluate the effectiveness of influencer marketing campaign.

Here are some important KPIs and metrics to think about:

Reach: Determine the number of followers or users that have seen your influencer marketing campaign.

Reach gives an idea of the overall reach and the potential size of its audience.

Engagement: Determine the extent of the engagement among your audience through the campaign.

These can be metrics that include comments, likes and shares. It can also include saves, likes and click-throughs.

The metrics of engagement indicate the success of the campaign at grabbing and keeping the attention of an audience.

Impressions: Keep track of the amount of times that your content from the campaign was presented to viewers.

Impressions can provide insight on the possibility of exposure for your site and how much of exposure it has gotten.

Check for conversions and clicks. Monitor the amount of clicks that are made on links in your campaign and monitor sales, like purchases registrations, downloads, or sign-ups.

The metrics above demonstrate the effectiveness of the campaign to influence users to take action and help you attain your goals.

Hashtag performance and Brand Mentions Check the frequency of brand mentions as well as the impact and engagement of specific hashtags for campaigns.

These numbers show how the campaign's influence on the visibility of brands, their audience participation, as well as the efficacy of strategies using hashtags.

Website traffic and referrals Examine the volume of traffic generated on your website by influencer marketing referrals.

Monitor the source of traffic for particular influencers or platforms to assess the success of your advertising campaign at driving site visits.

The growth of your audience and the acquisition of followers Track the increase in your social media followers and keep track of the number of new followers gained over the duration of the campaign.

These indicators reflect your campaigns' ability to grow your reach and draw new followers.

Sentiment Analysis: Conduct a sentiment analysis to assess the general opinion and sentiment surrounding your campaign.

Check the positive, negative and neutral reactions that is associated with the campaign in order to determine the response of the public and assess the brand's credibility.

Determine KPIs and metrics that are aligned with the goals of your campaign and give you insight into the effectiveness on engagement, reach, and impact of your influencer marketing campaigns.

Instruments for Monitoring and Tracking the Performance

Using tools to track and evaluating the results of your marketing campaign involving influencers makes it easier to collect and analyze data.

These are some tools that could aid in the monitoring and tracking of campaign performance:

Social Media Analytics Tools: Make use of built-in analytics for social media platforms like Instagram Insights, YouTube Analytics or Twitter Analytics.

These tools offer valuable insight on engagement, reach, the demographics of audiences, as well as how content performs on each of the platforms.

Influencer marketing platforms: A lot of influencer marketing platforms provide the ability to track and analyze campaign performance. They also give a complete report on the performance of campaigns.

They aggregate the data of multiple influencers making it possible to keep track of the reach, engagement, as well as other important metrics all together.

URL Shorteners as well as UTM Parameters: Make use of URL shorteners, like Bitly as well as Google URL Shortener, to generate trackable links to your influencer marketing campaign. Include UTM parameters in URLs so that you can track media, source of traffic and the name of your campaign.

It allows you to monitor precisely the conversions and traffic to your campaign.

Google Analytics: Integrate Google Analytics into your website to monitor campaign-specific user traffic, conversions and the behavior of users.

Create goals and funnels for evaluating the efficiency of influencer-driven traffic to achieve your goals.

Social Listening Instruments: Make use of tools for social listening, for example Brandwatch, Sprout Social, or Hootsuite Insights to track and analyse social media interactions in connection with your brand or campaign.

These tools can help you identify brand comments, moods and new trends.

Survey and Feedback Tools: Conduct polls or gather feedback from your customers for gathering qualitative data as well as insight into their opinions about your campaign to influencers.

Tools such as SurveyMonkey and Google Forms can help you make and distribute surveys quickly.

Pick tools that meet your goals for the campaign, offer all the required information, and allow for effective monitoring and tracking of results.

Analysis of Data and Extracting Information

Data analysis from influencer marketing campaigns is essential in gaining actionable information.

This is how you can effectively evaluate information from campaigns:

Data Consolidation: Combine information that comes from multiple sources like social media websites, analytics, as well as the influencer marketing platforms.

Combining quantitative information, like reach, engagement and conversions, together along with qualitative information, like sentiment analysis, and feedback.

Comparative Analyses: Compare campaign performance across different content formats, influencers platforms, influencers, or campaigns.

Chapter 13: Staying Ahead In The Evolving Influencer The Landscape

In this rapidly changing world of influencer marketing, it's essential to be on top of the latest the latest trends in the industry, and be able to adapt to adjustments in algorithms used by social media be aware of influencer fraud, establish authentic connections, and discover new and emerging platforms.

In this section we'll explore ways that will help you keep afloat with the ever-changing market of influencers.

Staying Current with the Latest Industry Trends and best practices

Being aware of industry trends and the best practices is crucial to stay ahead of the world of influencer marketing.

Here are a few strategies to keep you on track:

Industry Blogs and Publications Read reputable journals and blogs that provide market trends, news and research study.

Keep up-to-date with the latest developments techniques, strategies, and new techniques to improve your skills and keep you on top of the game.

Take part in events and conferences Take part in conferences and events for influencers or seminars as well as webinars to learn from experts in the field and thinkers.

The events offer valuable networking opportunities, and also allow attendees to take advantage of the most successful campaigns as well as industry trends in person.

Sign up to Professional Networks: Join professional networks and groups that are focused on marketing that is influenced by influencers.

Join discussions discuss experiences, engage in discussions, and exchange ideas with your peers within the field.

These social networks allow you for people to share their knowledge as well as keep you informed of the latest fashions.

Follow influential people and key industry players: Follow influential people as well as brands and other major industry players on the Social media sites.

Take note of the contents they publish, the collaborations that they participate in, as well as the strategies they use.

It helps you keep up-to-date on trends in the industry as well as inspire your own campaign.

Continuous Learning and Education You should invest in continual learning and training to increase your understanding of influencer marketing.

You can enroll in online courses and workshops or get certifications with in-depth information and insight.

Keep an open mind and be curious to innovative ideas and approaches.

Staying informed of the latest the latest trends in the industry and top techniques, you are able to modify your strategy, adopt creative strategies and retain an edge in your market.

Responding to the changing social Media Algorithms

The algorithms for social media are continuously changing, affecting the visibility and reach of the content created by influencers.

How to adjust to the changes in algorithmic algorithms for social media:

Stay informed about Algorithm Changes: Keep an eye on the latest announcements and news on social media sites concerning algorithm updates.

Keep up-to-date with platform blogs, official accounts, or even newsletters for updates on changes that could influence the success of your influencer marketing campaigns.

Diversify Your Platform Presence: Maintain an active presence on multiple social media sites.

This decreases the need to rely on a single platform. It also can help reduce the effects of algorithmic shifts.

Keep yourself informed of your strengths as well as weaknesses on every platform, and adapt your strategy to suit your needs.

Engage with relevant content: Connect with relevant posts via social media in order to increase the chance of your content being read.

Share, like, and comment or save content that is in line with your brand's image and the people who are part of your.

Engage in discussions and develop relationships with influencers and their fans.

Use Paid Adverts: Make use of ads that you pay for through social media to enhance the exposure and impact of your influencer campaign.

Utilize targeted advertising for specific audiences to increase the effectiveness of collaborations.

Optimize Content to Algorithms Be aware of the best ways to optimize content in order to be compatible with algorithmic requirements for social media. Know the ranking factors specific to each platform like relevance, engagement or the time of publication.

Maximize influencer-related content by engaging users, using appropriate hashtags and publishing in the most optimal time.

Try and test: Always try out different methods and experiments to determine how algorithm modifications impact your influencer marketing campaigns.

Review performance indicators and modify your strategy based on information and insight you collect.

Through adapting to modifications in the algorithms of social media You can increase the reach and visibility of your influencer marketing campaigns making sure they be a hit with the people you want to reach.

The art of navigating Influencer Fraud, Fake Engagement

Fraud in influencers and fake engagement are major challenges for the world of influencer marketing.

Here are some strategies that can aid you with these problems:

Due diligence and thorough research Perform thorough research before selecting the influencers you want to work with for your campaigns. Examine their posts, content, performance metrics, audience demographics as well as previous collaborations.

Be on the lookout for indicators of suspect activities, like sudden increases in engagement or followers.

Check for authenticity: Search for indications of authenticity the influencer's posts and interactions.

True influencers usually display an unwavering tone, top-quality material, and genuine interaction with their fans. Check comments, likes and shares to evaluate the legitimacy of their interactions.

Utilize Influencer Marketing Platforms Make use of influencer marketing platforms with built-in fraud detection and verification methods.

The platforms employ algorithms and data analysis to detect fraud and fake engagements.

A partnership with an established platform reduces the possibility of falling prey to fraudulent influencers.

Influencer Auditing Tools: Use tools for auditing the influence of an individual for example, Social Blade or HypeAuditor, to determine the legitimacy of an influencer's follower and their engagement.

These programs analyze patterns in data and offer insight into possible criminal activity or suspicious behavior.

Set up Authenticity Parameters: Create standards and criteria to assure authenticity when working with influencers.

Promoting transparency and ethical conduct like disclosing paid content, staying clear of fraudulent methods as well as encouraging genuine interaction.

The Influencer Agreement and Contracts Incorporate clauses into your agreements and contracts with influencers which address fraud by influencers and false engagement.

It is important to clearly define expectations about transparency, authenticity, as well as the consequences of fraud practices.

Through proactive actions to avoid influencer fraud and false engagement, you will be able to ensure your brand's credibility and maintain trust with your customers, and guarantee the efficacy of your influencer marketing strategies.

Establishing authentic and long-term relationships

The development of authentic and lasting relations with influencers is vital for lasting and effective influencer marketing.

This is how you can foster these connections:

Choose the right influencers Select influencers whose beliefs the content they share and their the audience are in line with yours.

Seek out long-term possibilities as well as shared goals.

The genuine relationship between your company and influential people is the basis for a genuine and successful relationship.

Reach out to Influencers: When you reach out to influential people, tailor your outreach.

Show that you've done your homework and display your genuine interest in their work.

Create collaboration plans that are tailored on their strengths, and the needs of their target.

Develop mutually beneficial partnerships: Develop a mutually beneficial partnership with influential people.

Give them opportunities to succeed and develop by offering exclusive collaborations with content or access to brand new products or participation with brand-related initiatives.

Provide ongoing assistance, direction as well as feedback to assist you achieve your goals.

Engage Beyond Campaigns: Interact with influencers in a way that goes beyond the specific campaign.

Engage with their work and share their work as well as engage in conversation.

Give them a special thanks for their efforts and acknowledge their accomplishments.

The ability to build a lasting relationship is more than just a transactional partnership.

Collaboration on Content Creation: Collaboration with influencers and other stakeholders to create content.

Participate in the brainstorming process, ask for their opinions and let them have creative control within the brand's guidelines.

The co-creation of content helps foster authenticity and ownership, which strengthens the relationship between brands and influencers.

Communication and Transparency: Keep clear and honest contact with those who influence you.

Be sure to inform them of goals, guidelines for campaigns, and performance indicators.

Provide feedback and address any problems or issues immediately.

Through the development of authentic, long-term connections with influential people to establish the credibility of your brand, capitalize on the influence of their followers, and be successful in the long-term with the field of influencer marketing.

Explore new and emerging platforms

As the landscape of influencers changes the new and emerging platforms provide the possibility of innovation while also reaching an untapped market.

Learn how to use different platforms efficiently:

Investigate Emerging Platforms: Stay updated on new social media platforms, applications or other technologies getting attention.

Find out their demographics for users along with engagement trends and the possibility of the influencer of marketing.

Assess their relevancy to the target market and the goals of your brand.

Test pilot campaigns Test pilot campaigns using new platforms in order to evaluate their effectiveness as well as gauge the reaction of the public.

Begin with smaller-scale collaborations or campaigns to test the potential of the platform before investing large amounts of money.

Work in partnership with Early Adopter Influencers: Identify influential individuals who have been early adopters of the latest platforms.

Partner with them to gain their experience and gain insight about the features that make this platform unique and user preferences.

Influencers from early adopters can offer useful advice and guidance to help use the platform efficiently.

Track Engagement and Performance Monitoring the performance and participation of your campaigns using different platforms.

Examine the response of your audience to engagement and other metrics as well as your platform's capacity to meet the objectives of your campaign.

Modify your strategies in light of research and data.

Be Innovative: Accept the latest innovations and formats for content that are created on the different platforms.

Try out live streaming, video and AR, augmented reality (AR) or other interactive elements that attract audiences in innovative ways.